# The Twilight Mind

## Twilight Saga Psychology Skills

WHAT PEOPLE ARE SAYING ABOUT

# THE TWILIGHT MIND

*A fascinating read. I really relate the book's ideas to my three grown up children as well as myself. This book will help you to make better choices, give you hope, and show you other important lessons from the* Twilight Saga.

**Susan Markby**, Mother, University Student, Twilight Fan

*The snappy and novel use of best-practice self-help information is delightful.*

**Andrew Domoney**, Registered Nurse

*An empowering and user-friendly text that promotes confidence, independence and smart survival strategies. A useful tool for educators to help students develop positive life skills.*

**Stephen Lippingwell**, B (Econ), Dip (Ed), Masters (Ed Admin), AIMM. Head of Social Sciences, Queensland Secondary School. Public School Educator (20 years)

*Anyone who's into Twilight can now gain rich insights and the best psychology skills to empower themselves. As a parent and a youth worker, I believe this book will be an invaluable self-improvement tool for many people.*

**Paul Leonardi**, Youth Worker (Youth Link), Parent

*My customers will really enjoy this interesting psychological interpretation of the* Twilight Saga. *The Twilight series is big in Russia and Ukraine. I feel this book, which interprets their folklore and myths, will be very popular.*

**Yuri Tkach**, Manager, Bayda Books (Ukrainian/Russian Book Supplier)

# The Twilight Mind

## Twilight Saga Psychology Skills

Dr Julie-Anne Sykley

BOOKS

Winchester, UK
Washington, USA

First published by O-Books, 2012
O-Books is an imprint of John Hunt Publishing Ltd., Laurel House, Station Approach,
Alresford, Hants, SO24 9JH, UK
office1@o-books.net
www.o-books.com

For distributor details and how to order please visit the 'Ordering' section on our website.



ISBN: 978 1 78099 101 6



A CIP catalogue record for this book is available from the British Library.

Design: Stuart Davies

Printed in the USA by Edwards Brothers Malloy

This book is not authorized by or associated with any persons, publishers or producers of the Twilight Saga novels or films.
Neither is it a substitute for professional health advice, diagnosis or treatment. People with serious health concerns should always seek advice from qualified health providers.

# CONTENTS

*For my beautiful mum, Motra Cherednek*
*Every day we are closer to each other.*
*I love you forever and forever.*
*Your favorite baby always, Julia XXX*

# Acknowledgements

Thank you John Hunt, Trevor Greenfield, Kate Rowlandson and team at John Hunt Publishing for believing in this book. I tried to mesmerize you – and it worked!

I am deeply grateful to each special individual who cared enough to provide comments about this book – you shine!

Thank you to the author and creator of the Twilight Saga, Stephenie Meyer, for sharing such a wonderful dream.

I sincerely acknowledge the wisdom, beauty, and nature-wise creativity of Quileute legend and Ukrainian folklore. I hope I have done an adequate job rejuvenating these two powerful cultures that neither time nor tyranny have been able to quell.

*In the forest, after twilight*
*In the coldest darkest gloom*
*Underneath the ice-bright starlight*
*Waits the brooding vampire groom.*

*When moonlight, at midnight*
*Meets the top-most, wind-tossed branches*
*The girl who dreams at night*
*Entranced, takes on her chances.*

*Fire, in one wolf's heart, burns higher*
*But the vampire's shadow blocks all bright,*
*Beast and beast, locked in battle*
*Fight for desire, but who will bite?*

Answer: It is the *girl* who takes a healthy 'bite' out of life, psychologically speaking. In the Twilight Saga novels, the main character, Bella Swan, makes positive choices that will change destiny. As you can, too.

# A Taste

## Twilight's Hidden Power

The Twilight Saga is an exciting vampire romance that has become a worldwide book and film phenomenon. Stephenie Meyer's hit novels *Twilight, New Moon, Eclipse,* and *Breaking Dawn* have received attention and adoration from millions of people around the globe. Why does an icy place like Forks set the world on fire? Well, this fantasy series is a brilliant love story – a dark and daring, brooding and bloody *Romeo and Juliet*. It's a supernatural story too. Otherworldly forces – vampires, werewolves, strange 'gifts' – add extra eerie mystique. And the plot's a twister. In particular, Edward is a vampire with an awfully good heart . . . even if it doesn't beat or pump blood. So, is that it? As if!

Behind the forbidden romance, the paranormal action, the literary craftiness, intriguing references to classic literature, history, music and more, the Twilight series masks another exciting world. It's a world of utmost importance. It's a world that embraces both darkness and light, courage and fear, love and hate, and life and death. It's a world that acknowledges dreams and desires, thoughts and feelings, deeds and choices, the peaks of happiness and the pits of misery. It's the crux of the thrill . . . It's a Twilight Saga X-factor . . . It's what helps good to beat evil in the end . . . It's the powerful world of *psychology*!

## What this book is *not*

Anyone can write about Twilight Saga flaws, faults, weaknesses, what a bad influence this racy vampire story is on teens – and condemn Meyer's popular novels that get people reading. After all, aren't neck attacks and (blood) bank robberies up among 17-year-olds in *your* town? As I am a psychologist, I could easily give you juicy and convincing gossip about Bella's borderline personality, Edward's stalking behavior and other sick themes. And what would that achieve? A bitter view of the Twilight books. An improvement in people's ability to complain and pay attention to the bad side of things. Hey, it might even help people establish a super-strong negative cognitive style. In my opinion, there are more than enough critics, conflicts, and problems out there already. What makes *this* book about the Twilight world different is that it does not devalue Meyer's series nor does it bully Bella. Naw, this book is none of that.

## What *is* this book? What will it help you to achieve?

This book hunts for Twilight Saga strengths and its best-ever psychological ideas and strategies, which are worth bringing to your attention. This book strives to identify the most valuable psychological material in the Twilight novels to increase your insight and improve your life.

With help from Bella, Edward, Jacob and the fantastic world of Twilight, this book will help you to:

- Achieve powerful psychological insights into Twilight Saga adventures and characters
- Learn psychological ideas which you can use to make a positive difference in your life
- Unlock the power of your extraordinary mind
- Develop super-effective mental-health Skills4Life!

Not only will you discover the Twilight Saga's underlying psychological allure, you will gain powerful knowledge about yourself – your deepest desires, your darkest feelings, your best possible potential. With help from mesmerizing Twilight adventures and psychologically instructive werewolves and vampires, are you ready to re-vamp your insight?

1

# I Dream: Let's Get Unconscious

*Let the vampire's creaking wing*
*Hide the stars while banshees sing*
*Let the ghouls gorge all night long*
*Dreams will keep you safe and strong.*
- Thomas Pynchon, novelist

## Twilight's Unconscious Action

As soon as you step inside the Twilight Saga fantasy world, you also enter the unseen world of the unconscious mind. After all, Stephenie Meyer's inspiration for a vampire romance did come to her in a dream: 'I had a dream about the characters that would later become Bella and Edward. It was such a vivid and wonderful dream that I didn't want to forget it. And so I wrote and wrote' (Stephenie Meyer, *The Twilight Journals*).

Deep inside everyone, there lies incredible mental power – drives, desires, determination, and more – that shifts and shapes our behavior. As leading lady Bella Swan tells it: 'Aware even in unconsciousness that he was there – I slept free of nightmares' (*Eclipse*, p185). While Bella is asleep, her unconscious mind reassures her of a settling presence in the room – her vampire sweetheart Edward.

Why so much covert mental action in the Twilight series? What is so special about the unconscious mind anyway? Do Meyer's books awaken our own unconscious longings? Is that why the world loves Twilight? So many questions, but only one way to get answers. Let's get unconscious inside the Twilight zone . . .

## The Wild Mind

In the Twilight Saga, unconscious mental power appears in the very first pages of book one on Bella's first day of school. Bella is mysteriously drawn to one thing only. Something beautiful, dangerous, and forbidden: Edward the vampire. As Bella explains: 'It was there, sitting in the lunchroom, trying to make conversation with seven curious strangers, that I first saw them . . . and then his dark eyes flickered to mine' (*Twilight*, p17). An intriguing unconscious first reaction, don't you think? Perhaps Dr Sigmund Freud – the infamous Austrian psychoanalyst and the first person to put forward a theory about the unconscious mind – can provide some inside insights into such mysterious mental affairs.

According to Freud's psychological theory, the mind is like an 'iceberg' floating in the water. Only a small part of the conscious mind – the tip of the iceberg – is visible above the water. The remaining 90% of the mind, the unconscious, exists unseen beneath the surface. The unconscious mind is well beyond the reach of the conscious mind – it contains ideas, thoughts, impulses and urges that we are not aware of. Yet, these unconscious forces are always influencing and motivating our behavior. The influence of the unconscious mind is so powerful that William James (the founder of American psychology) called it the most important find of the century.

In Freud's view, Bella's 'first sight' of Edward definitely suggests her unconscious mind at work. Bella's instant attraction to Edward would be due to some deep desire, unmet need, or unresolved issue that she is yet to figure out. On the whole, Freud's view is that humans are much like newborn vampires. They're selfish creatures driven by aggressive impulses, urges for pleasure that need instant gratification, and a desire to express unruly sexual behavior. To thrive and survive in society, however, people must control their top secret drives. But that's pretty hard when people are born with a primitive mental core that Freud calls the *id*.

## The Impulsive Id

The id – our unconscious mind – only wants to satisfy wild and impulsive urges. For example, the id would want you to have sex in the Volterra city plaza at noon, right in front of the clock tower for everyone to see – behavior which is considered socially outrageous, unacceptable *and* unlawful. To stop people from embarrassing themselves and going completely berzerk, the conscious mind tries to control and repress these intense urges. And that's when it happens: inner conflict inside your mind.

## A Three-Way Split

To keep the eager and impatient *id* under control, Freud says that the human mind develops a conscious *ego* and a *superego*. The ego is the normal thinking mind and it tries to satisfy the id safely or reduce its pain if it can't be immediately gratified. It also listens to the superego (our conscience), a moral part of the mind that tells us what is right or wrong and helps us to adapt to the civilized world. As the Twilight Saga suggests in various adventures, the id, ego and superego are always in conflict with each other. Consider Edward's mental plight, for example: 'I wrestled all night, while watching you sleep, with the chasm between what I knew was *right*, moral, ethical, and what I *wanted*' (*Twilight*, p265).

Deep down in his mind, Edward *wants* to bite Bella, but his higher conscious mind *knows* this would be wrong. As you can see here, Edward's ego and superego are keeping the lid on his id.

## The Surreal Mind

Different adventures from the Twilight series allude to other psychological theories about the unconscious. The famous Swiss psychotherapist Carl Jung introduced ideas from myth, alchemy, spirituality, Eastern philosophy, and the supernatural to explain the unconscious mind. Jung wrote that the unconscious is the mind's 'nocturnal side' and it involves 'psychic activity which we apprehend as dreamlike fantasy'. Jung's approach explains mysterious adventures such as Bella's dreamlike hike in the forest:

> I didn't realize how much more efficiently I was moving . . . I wasn't even starting to look around for it yet. And then, with an abruptness that disoriented me, I stepped through a low arch made by two vine maples – pushing past the chest-high ferns – into the meadow.
>
> (*New Moon*, p233)

In this forest scene, Bella's unconscious mind leads her to her favorite meadow in a surreal and dreamlike way. What's more, Bella's hike shows how the innermost mind guides behavior. It pursues our heart's desires and takes us to special places, even if we aren't 'looking around' much or paying close attention to our surroundings, exactly as Bella describes it. Bella's unconscious mind has lured her to a meadow that means a lot to her. Bella's unconscious mental power, a deep and dreamy mental GPS system, would really impress Jung!

### A Mental Art Gallery

As Bella's dreams, fancies, fears and fantasies throughout the Twilight books suggest, the unconscious mind is like a colorful and lively 'art gallery'. It is a lavish collection of images – imaginative and provocative mental creations and masterpieces that move you, motivate you and affect your mood and behavior. The unconsciousness is a secret epic pic file!

### A Dreamy Double

According to Jung's theory, the unconscious mind has two mental art galleries: 1) A *personal* one that has unique images created only by the individual and 2) A *collection* of creative works submitted by many human contributors from the past. Jung's theory can provide deep insight into the minds of important Twilight characters.

## The personal unconscious

This part of the mind is said to have collected ideas and images throughout an individual's personal lifespan. It contains beautiful dreams, forgotten memories, hidden fears and many other private ideas. Consider the minds of these important Twilight characters:

- Carlisle would surely hide away many memories about his cruel and strict father somewhere in his unconscious. As Carlisle himself explains, the psychological experience of his father's brutality is what drove Carlisle to be so compassionate and heal others in the first place (*New Moon*, p36).
- Alice's painful experiences in an abusive 1920s asylum are likely to be buried deep inside her mind. It makes psychological sense for Alice to develop a happy, bubbly and enthusiastic personality to minimize further emotional pain and to compensate for past emotional deprivation – even if she is not fully conscious of this development.
- Rosalie's unconscious mind would possess traumatic and terrifying memories of the time she was brutally murdered by her fiancé and his gang. No wonder Rosalie gets so upset about Bella's decision to become a vampire. It probably reminds Rosalie's unconscious mind of the day her human life was stolen from her, along with the lifestyle choices she could no longer make.
- Jasper would have stored away disturbing war memories deep inside his unconscious mind. At times, these

thoughts might escape and resurface as frightening flashbacks or nightmarish visions.

## The collective unconscious

This part of the mind is said to contain ideas and images that have been collected throughout the history of humanity. Jung believes that the mind inherits all the collective psychological experiences of humankind over time. What's more, this mental art gallery of accrued wisdom from the minds of people in the past guides and directs people's current behavior. In the Twilight Saga, the Quileute community would have a very well-developed 'collective unconscious':

- The Native American Quileute people have passed down important information for many generations. This includes their creation tale that they originally descended from wolves.
- At an unconscious mental level, characters like Jacob would probably dream often about wolves. He would also react and relate strongly to wolves without really knowing why.
- Wolves would be 'on Jacob's mind' a lot because wolves are such an important part of his ancestry, Quileute culture, the history of his people, and the forest environment. In fact, the Twilight series does suggest that wolves are deeply embedded in Jacob's mind in the form of 'scary'and 'chilling' stories and pictures (*Twilight*, p106–108).

As Jung's theory suggests and Jacob's mind illustrates, the 'wolf' is just one of many powerful images that dwells deep inside the collective human unconscious. Of course, the reason why people like us are so fascinated by vampires and werewolves is because the same powerful images lurk deep inside our collective mental galleries too, stirred to life by stories like the Twilight Saga.

## The Name 'Swan': An Unconscious Slip?

As all Twilight fans know backwards in their deepest unconscious sleep, Bella's surname is 'Swan'. But does this word mean something? Is it perhaps an author's crafty and conscious tip? Or just an innocent, unplanned, and unconscious 'Freudian' slip? Or a bit of both? While 'Swan' *may* have been a totally random word-choice, this word also seems to have loads of covert meaning. In any case, there are enough intriguing clues to increase suspicion about Bella Swan's surname.

### Swan clue # 1 – pure and powerful

The swan is a beautiful bird and a powerful symbol in many cultures. According to the *Dictionary of Symbols, Myths and Legends*, the white swan symbolizes 'purity and perfection' in Asia and Europe. This seems to fit with Bella's personality, which is pure (she accepts vampires, believes Edward is good and says he has a soul) and powerful (Bella has the strength to save others and the willpower to pursue her goals).

### Swan clue # 2 – nice neck

A *swan* does have an attractive and pleasing neck. And so does a *Swan* . . . especially to a thirsty vampire. Maybe Bella's surname is Swan because swans have lovely S-curved necks and human necks tempt vampires. The neck is possibly the most important body part in romantic *and* scary scenes in the Twilight Saga. Bella's neck is an intimate part of her body that Edward kisses but must never bite.

### Swan clue # 3 – in love

Swans are famous symbols of love and romance. So the name 'Swan' may be a tip to Bella and Edward's love for each other. After all, when two swans face each other, their S-curved necks make a lovely 'heart' shape. Throughout history, there are many beautiful pictures of swans posed in this manner. And when two swans love each other, they intertwine their long lean necks with each other, which adds extra 'neck' meaning.

**Swan clue # 4 – William Shakespeare**

Another reason the word 'swan' may have special meaning in the Twilight Saga is because the books refer to the medieval works of William Shakespeare, and Edward and Bella's love story echoes Shakespeare's play *Romeo and Juliet*. Adding to this, Greek myth says that swans contain the souls of great poets, writers and musicians such as Shakespeare. That is why Shakespeare is called the Swan of Avon, after the river that runs through his birthplace.

**Swan clue # 5 – sweet ways**

Swans are sweet, sensitive, tender, peace-loving birds. This accurately reflects the sweetie-pie personality features of Bella and Edward.

**Swan clue # 6 – sad song**

A swan's cry is 'a song of love and death', says the *Dictionary of Symbols, Myths and Legends.* The phrase 'swan song' (the song that a dying swan sings) means 'the last appearance, publication, or exhibition' by a writer, artist, or public figure. Since Bella loves Edward and wants to die so that she can be with him forever as a vampire, her deadly plan is much like a dying swan song.

**Swan clue # 7 – the fairytale factor**

This may be the juiciest swan theory of all. Bella starts off as a lost, sad and plain human girl who eventually turns into a vampire diva, right? Well, this sure is reminiscent of a famous children's fairytale. The story 'The Ugly Duckling' is about a young dull-looking bird that grows into a 'beautiful swan'. In Italian, *bella* means 'beautiful' and in the Twilight series it's 'Bella' who becomes the '*beautiful* Swan'. What's more, this swan theory is psychologically empowering because it suggests that tremendous *change* is possible in life. If people put their mind to it, they can progress from nothing to something, from despair to happiness, and from powerlessness to power to reach a great and powerful swan state.

## How the Unconscious Communicates

## What Do Twilight's Colors Mean?

The original Twilight books have striking black, white and red covers. But what do these three colors suggest psychologically? How much do they relate to the plot? A lot, especially when it involves Bella Swan. You see, the unconscious mind likes to communicate in *symbols*. A symbol is an idea, image, sign, shape, or metaphor that represents or means something else. In the Twilight books, black, white and red are not just colors, they describe stages of change in Bella's psychological journey.

### Black

The color black often points to negative psychological experiences. According to *Dictionary of Symbols, Myths and Legends*, black is often associated with evil, difficulty and death. It suggests gloom, doom, depression, wickedness, cruelty, and dark and disturbing ideas. Sometimes, black has positive meanings. The brightness of light, or mental enlightenment for example, can only appear in darkness. In the *nigredo* or black phase of alchemy, the alchemist must sacrifice everything and give up all worldly attachments in order to be reborn as a more powerful being.

### Bella's 'Black' Doubts

In the Twilight series, black depicts Bella's dark and difficult psychological journey ahead. Sometimes, people must face negative challenges in life, which can make the path ahead look confusing and unclear. The only way to escape the darkness is to look within for bright ideas and wise solutions. Bella must therefore embark on an inner journey of self-discovery. She must look deep inside her mind and heart – the darkness within the darkness – to resolve her doubts and despair. To escape the human life that Bella feels brings her spirits down, depresses her and traps her, Bella must examine her dreams, follow her heart and listen to her inner voice. Only then can Bella dissolve her black uncertainty with the white light of clarity, and find inner peace.

## White

White suggests positive psychological experiences to the mind. The color white means 'purity, innocence, and perfection' says the *Dictionary of Symbols, Myths and Legends*. Since white light comprises all the colors of the spectrum, white embraces unity. It also symbolizes the soul after it has been delivered from the torments of the flesh and passion. Psychological qualities such as innocence, peace, justice, truth, transparency and incorruptibility are linked to white. Since white hair is a mark of old age, white stands for honor, wisdom, and compassion too. The *albedo* or white phase in alchemy is the purifying stage. An alchemist becomes pure by relinquishing earthly desires or selfish behaviors. In the Twilight books, Bella's goal to be a vampire intensifies and purifies. She gives up her desire to be human as she becomes more and more determined to become a vampire.

## Bella's 'White' Insight

In the Twilight books, Bella's psychological journey changes from black to white. That is, from confusion to clarity, ignorance to wisdom, pain to peace, human to supernatural, and innocence to power. At first, Bella is an innocent young girl, a naive little lamb who knows nothing about the dangerous world of vampirism. Bella is also a miserable human (this is her psychological blackness). After meeting Edward, Bella steadily acquires knowledge, understanding, experience, and happiness in relation to other worlds and possible directions in life. Once Bella decides she really does love Edward and wants to be a vampire, her white wisdom and bright insight dispel her dark doubts. After that, Bella achieves white psychological power. She becomes a content individual, a competent vampire, and a successful warrior in the *Breaking Dawn* war. She embraces all the white virtues of maturity – truth, compassion, wisdom, honor and peace. In fact, Bella rises to the powerful rank of a white queen, the 'white chess piece' suggested on the *Breaking Dawn* book cover.

### Red

To the human mind, red suggests psychological energy and expression. It relates to ideas like action, vitality, creativity, desire, passion, excitement, and emotion. According to a dictionary on myth, red is 'the colour of life, fire, blood and vital energy'. Red denotes life because blood is a life force that runs through the veins of humans and animals. Since blood is red, this makes red a *sacred* and *secret* color. 'Sacred' because ancient people linked blood to the soul – people who lose too much blood also lose their lives. 'Secret' because the blood that flows through veins and arteries is invisible, hidden beneath skin and flesh. Sometimes red means death. A red sunset signals a dying day while a large blood loss can kill a bleeding victim. In the *rubedo* or red phase the alchemist is now cleansed and no longer attached to earthly life and the chains that hold one back. When people are 'in the red', they are ready to reach their best possible selves.

### Bella's 'Red' Strength

In the Twilight Saga, Bella's psychological journey has a red phase for a number of reasons. Red is the color of romance and passion, which reflects the true love that Bella and Edward develop for each other. Red also screams danger for Bella. Since vampires drink blood, Bella's sacred life force is always at risk from death. Since red also means action, energy, and sacrifice, these ideas further paint Bella's experience red – Bella makes some pretty serious sacrifices to be with Edward and keep her loved ones safe. Bella's acts of passion and courage change the course of destiny, enabling two ill-fated lovers to be together forever in the end. Bella's love, strength, and selfless behavior suggest red-hot adventure and a sizzling psychological makeover.

## Secret Slavic Sorcery

Did you know that in East Europe – where vampire legends are so old that they originate in pagan times – the colors black, white and red are linked to Slavic sorcery? According to an ancient myth from Ukraine, a fabulous creature lives in the deepest, darkest and wildest forests – a dark Goddess called *Baba Yaha*. This all-seeing sorceress commands otherworldly servants, including a White Knight who is dawn, a Red Knight who is day, and a Black Knight who is night. These three colors represent 'personal transformation', which Baba Yaha rules. Black suggests the death of old ways, old fears and ignorance. White stands for psychological purification and advancement after dark times. And red represents passion and the vital life force. In line with Slavic sorcery, Bella is energized by her true love for Edward (red), she leaves her old lifestyle behind (black), and she creates a new and happier world for herself as a vampire (white).

Just like Bella does in her Twilight world, one day you might wish to explore your inner depths and shed your old ways (black). Maybe you will discover your true passion (red) and explore a new path in life (white). In any case, if a wild wind begins to blow, the trees creak and groan, leaves start spinning through the air and you hear a swarm of spirits shriek and wail, take heed. Baba Yaha may be coming to see you.

## What Do Twilight's Cosmic Scenes Mean?

The book titles *Twilight*, *New Moon*, *Eclipse*, and *Breaking Dawn* are visually evocative, to say the least. In nature, 'twilight', 'dawn', a 'new moon', and an 'eclipse' indicate special times of the day or significant positions of the planets. But days, nights, the sun, the moon and stars aren't just astrophysical phenomena. They relate to psychological experiences, images that inhabit the unconscious mind.

Maybe you have noticed that the Twilight Saga's main characters – Bella, Edward, and Jacob – are described in solar, lunar and stellar ways. For example, after Edward broke up with Bella, she described herself as 'a lost moon' that no longer had an earth to orbit, circling meaninglessly in empty space (*New Moon*, p201). Psychologically, Edward was 'the world' to Bella, so when he left her it felt like the whole planet went missing. As for Jacob, he is a happy and sunny character: 'Jacob was simply a perpetually happy person . . . like an earthbound sun, whenever someone was within his gravitational pull, Jacob warmed them' (*New Moon*, p145). As for Edward's thoughts about Bella, she is his shooting star in this favorite quote among Twilighters:

> Before you, Bella, my life was like a moonless night. Very dark . . . And then you shot across my sky like a meteor. Suddenly everything was on fire; there was brilliancy, there was beauty . . . My eyes were blinded by the light.
> (*New Moon*, p514)

As these scenes suggest, the Twilight Saga's outer universe also says a lot about *inner* experience.

The psychiatrist Dr Thomas Wehr, a psychobiology researcher and a leading authority on environmental influences on behavior, says that nature's intervals – such as night, day, dawn, twilight and lunar phases – are cosmic events that affect psychological experience. According to science, night and day embrace two different worlds – a cosmic one and a psychological one. Maybe that is why the Twilight Saga cosmos does such a wonderful job of describing Bella's inner cosmos.

## Bella's Inner Cosmos

### The Sun

To the unconscious mind, the sun represents rationality, public identify and the outer world. The bright and strong power of the sun suggests worldly success and bright, clear and sure social directions in life.

### Bella's experience

Jacob – with his warm, glowing and beaming nature – is Twilight Saga's 'sun' character. In contrast, Bella is not a sunny person. She is not especially confident, outgoing, cheerful or emotionally expressive in public. Nor does she like to shine brightly in the social spotlight. Bella's disconnection from the sun is evident in her human life. As a human, Bella tends to be depressed, preoccupied in thought and socially withdrawn. Her inner cosmos is a dark and private place and her behavior is quite unsunlike.

### The Moon

As a symbol, the moon stands for the unconscious mind, inner emotional feelings and a person's mysterious side. The moon relates to dreams, the soul and renewal. This is because the moon disappears and then reappears in the sky during the lunar cycle. Moonlight often suggests inner enlightenment and the glow of spiritual power because it can guide a lost person on a dark night – through 'darkness and difficulty', that is.

### Bella's experience

Bella's psychological life fits well with moon meanings. For example, Bella dwells a lot in the unconscious realm of dreams, desires, and doubts. Her psychological journey ahead is dark and difficult – she is a somewhat depressed human who desperately wants to be with Edward forever. Just like moonlight on a dark night, her eventual choice – to become a vampire – lights her path ahead like moonlight.

## Twilight Time

Twilight is a peaceful and entrancing time of day. Due to the strange and ambient quality of light at this time, writers and artists call it the 'blue hour', after a French expression. The blue haze of twilight is a boundary point between day and night, darkness and light, and black and white. As such, twilight is a dividing-line that both *separates* and *joins* two opposite forces. The dim 'half-light' of twilight suggests the idea of being 'split' and 'suspended' in space (suspended like the Hanged Man in Tarot cards suggests). Of course, twilight can be a busy time when crepuscular creatures – such as crickets, dragonflies, owls and bats – hunt for food and become active.

To the human mind, twilight is romantic and tantalizing. It signals the onset of night, dark delights, sweet surprises and secret fantasies yet to be discovered and tasted (woo hoo). Edward and Bella clearly tap into these shadowy themes in telling chats like this one:

> 'It's twilight,' Edward murmured, looking at the western horizon . . . the end of another day, the return of the night. Darkness is so predictable, don't you think?' He smiled wistfully.
>
> 'I like the night. Without the dark, we'd never see the stars.'
>
> (*Twilight*, p204)

## Bella's experience

Just as twilight marks the end of an old day and lurks on the edge of a new night, Bella lingers on the verge of great psychological change. She seriously starts thinking about leaving her old human life behind and embarking on a brand new adventure in dark and uncharted personal territory – to become a vampire and be with Edward forever. Above all, Edward and Bella reach an 'impasse' in the *Twilight* novel. This is when Bella 'suspends' her decision to turn into a vampire, much like twilight hangs suspended between the light of day and the darkness of night.

### New Moon

A new moon means a new start. When the waxing crescent starts to build up into the full moon, this is the time to wish for what you want in life. This lunar phase is supposed to have the power to illuminate your heart's deepest desires. In East Europe, where vampires roam, ancient magic spells spoken at the appearance of a *molodyk* – a new moon – are believed to banish negative energy and attract positive energy from the all-powerful universe. As Pavilina Zolota's old Ukrainian moon spell suggests:

*New moon, silver-gold moon, dear,*
*Help, cleanse all,*
*Wash, bless [say person's name] here*
*To be healthy, happy and true*
*As bright and pure as you.*

Despite dark and difficult times in life (dark moon), people can always rebuild themselves, make a new start in life and be reborn (new moon).

### Bella's experience

'Tonight the sky was utterly black . . . A new moon. I shivered, though I wasn't cold' (*New Moon*, p75). Why would Bella shiver when it's not cold? Deep feelings of fear regarding a new, uncertain future without Edward, no doubt. However, just like a new moon rises out of a dark sky, Bella slowly rises from her dark despair after doing some serious soul-searching. She discovers new insights about herself and comes closer to understanding her innermost self. Just like a waxing crescent moon grows thicker and brighter over time, Bella grows psychologically wiser and stronger. A new moon (a bright crescent rising in a dark night sky) symbolizes Bella's growing love for Edward and her rise from dark uncertainty to psychological confidence.

## Dark Eclipse

An eclipse is a powerful cosmic junction and an important symbol to the unconscious mind. When the light from the sun or moon is masked by another planet, this produces a loss of light, brilliance or splendor. To eclipse another means to outshine, surpass or block something or someone. Sometimes, when the sun (the conscious self) and the moon (unconscious self) unite, this suggests a psychological union (the coming together of two unlike personal forces). But a full solar eclipse, which causes complete darkness, usually means a total 'eclipse' of reason by emotion.

## Bella's experience

When Jacob tells Bella: 'I would have been the air, the sun . . . But I can't fight with an eclipse' (*Eclipse*, p531), he means that he is like a sun that cannot compete with Edward. Bella's true love for Edward (who means 'the earth' to Bella) fully eclipses the bright and warm sunshine of Jacob's love. This masks Bella's ability to see Jacob's love for her. Bella's love for Edward completely and utterly eclipses Jacob's love and his chances of being with Bella.

## Bright Dawn

Dawn is the birth of a new day. To the unconscious mind, dawn suggests a new outlook or the 'dawning' of a new idea. It marks the disappearance or death of night and the arrival of the absolute power of light. In particular, dawn is the emergence of a new stage of life and a new understanding that involves leaving the darkness behind.

## Bella's experience

In the last book of the Twilight series, *Breaking Dawn*, Bella breaks free of her dark human misery, and breaks through to her psychological dawn. She finally becomes a vampire. Just as the day is born at dawn, Bella remarks, 'I had been born to be a vampire' in *Breaking Dawn* (p485). Furthermore, Bella is much brighter and happier as a supernatural creature, just as dawn is a lighter and brighter time of day.

(Source of meanings: Bowes, 1999; Eason, 2002; Colin, 2000; Lewis, 1995)

## What Dreams Mean

Messages from the unconscious mind appear in the weirdest ways and places. As the Twilight books suggest, unconscious ideas express themselves in daydreams, deeply relaxed states, and as visions. Above all, unconscious mental adventures like to come alive at night in the colorful world of dreams. Bella's dreams play a prominent role in the Twilight Saga, providing plenty of meaningful psychological information.

## What Are Dreams?

So what are dreams? What do they reveal about characters like Bella, or even ourselves? The newest approaches to dreams are neuroscientific – the latest studies are busy exploring links between dreams, genes, and brain plasticity. But to understand the underlying *meaning* of dreamscapes, one must refer back to the ever-famous psychoanalytic theories of Freud and Jung. To increase your insight into Bella's imaginative night life, you will need these psychological pointers to guide you through the world of dreams in the Twilight Saga.

### Dreams supply information

The most important point about dreams is that they supply information from the deep unconscious mind. This mysterious part of the mind is supposed to be easier to access when a person is deeply relaxed or asleep. Dr Sigmund Freud, who pioneered the psychoanalytical theory of dreams, maintained that 'dreams are the royal road to the unconscious'. The famous psychoanalyst Dr Carl Jung also asserted that 'the dream is specifically the utterance of the unconscious'. As Bella noticed waking up one morning: 'A dream trying to be remembered, struggled to break into my consciousness' (*Twilight*, p273).

### Dreams involve images

This world of dreams is a highly visual affair. According to the *Penguin Dictionary of Psychology,* dreams are defined as 'imagery during sleep'. A dream usually appears as a series of related or unrelated pictures, dredging up rich and dramatic images from a person's unconscious mind. In *New Moon,* Bella experienced 'strange, colourful dreams – dreams and nightmares – swirled dizzily around the inside of my head. They were so vivid. The horrible and the heavenly, all mixed together into a bizarre jumble' (p500).

### Dreams disguise data

Often, dreams 'code' and camouflage information, communicating messages indirectly – symbolically or metaphorically. This, says Freud, resolves feelings of guilt or embarrassment because it stops dreamers from having to face the true source of their anxiety. Bella's strange dream that a 'wolf growled at my feet' (*Twilight,* p114) can mean many things. Maybe Bella likes wolves. Maybe Bella's unconscious mind is trying to tell her that she feels threatened by someone's hostile verbal attacks. Maybe it is just a theatrical reminder for Bella not to lose her temper. However, a 'growl' can also relate to everyday phrases such as 'don't growl so much' (complain about things all the time). Or maybe Bella's dream is confirming her own hunches that a lot of spiritual and supernatural activity is happening around her.

### Dreams solve problems

Many people have the experience of being baffled by a particular problem, going to sleep, and then waking up with the answer. For example, a 19th-century chemist called F.A. Kekule once had a dream which is now famous. He was trying to figure out the shape of the benzene molecule. One night as Kekule was dozing in front of a fireplace, he saw snake structures in his mind: 'Long rows, sometimes more closely fitted together; all twining and twisting in snakelike motion. But look! What was that? One of the snakes had seized its own tail'. The image of a dancing snake grabbing its own tail and spinning around in a circle helped the chemist to solve a scientific problem – that the benzene molecule is arranged in 'a ring structure'. In the Twilight series, Bella's dream that 'a great russet wolf . . . stared intently at me, trying to convey something vital with his intelligent eyes' (*New Moon*, p292) helped Bella to figure out that Jacob is a shape-shifting wolf.

### Dreams guide behavior

Since dream images can have more than one meaning, Jung paid careful attention to various dream elements – images, subjects, storylines and solutions. One of Bella's dreams, for example, involves searching for something: 'I knew that if I found the beach, I would be able to see the sun' (*New Moon*, p290–291). Maybe this dream is trying to guide Bella towards happiness. Or maybe the 'sun' means knowledge, truth, or love to Bella. Only dreamers will know what their dreams really mean. That is why Jung often asked his own clients: 'What does the dream say to you?' Such questions helped people to understand their own personal dreams.

### Dreams suggest possibilities

A dream can reveal certain 'possibilities to be' for the first time to a dreamer. According to phenomenological psychologists Medard Boss and Erik Craig, dreams foreshadow one's potential by showing a range of possibilities safely within the dream state before the dreamer tests them out in reality. Such a dream can be a valuable decisive point in the life of a dreamer. For example, Bella was dreaming about something when suddenly 'the dream veered off course, like a train jumping the tracks' (*New Moon*, p292). Bella's dream about shape-shifting wolves that suddenly changes may have been trying to suggest that Bella can either continue to think or act along usual lines; or else she can explore the new path her dream is trying to show her – and experience new directions and possibilities in life.

## Bella's Dream Themes

According to the theories of Freud and Jung, dreams can have recurring themes. These have extra-special and significant meaning for dreamers. In the Twilight world, Bella repeatedly dreams about certain things, noted below.

- What might some of Bella's dream themes mean?
- What can these dreams tell us about Bella?
- What do these dreams reveal about Bella's directions in life?
- To help you develop some dream know-how, let's interpret Bella's very first dream . . .

## Darkness

> In my dream, it was very dark, and what dim light there was seemed to be radiating from Edward's skin. I couldn't see his face, just his back as he walked away from me, leaving me in the blackness. No matter how fast I ran, I couldn't catch up with him.
>
> (*Twilight*, p58)

Bella's very first dream in the Twilight Saga is about (guess who) Edward. It occurs soon after she meets the young mystery man at school. According to *The Dream Encyclopedia, darkness* in a dream can mean various things – evil, death, fear of the unknown, or feeling lost. It can also symbolize unconscious or unseen possibilities. The dream's atmosphere will determine which interpretation to make.

Although Bella's dream is 'very dark', it is not frightening. As such, the darkness in Bella's dream may suggest an 'uncertain' future with Edward at this time, an unresolved conflict in Bella's unconscious mind at this time. This dream also suggests that Bella may be infatuated by Edward and needs to understand him – because Bella wants to glow in his light, be with him, and see his face in the darkness. At an emotional level, this dream may be suggesting that Bella's romantic desires are awakening and that she is feeling attracted to Edward.

## Forests

'When I dreamed, I stood in the forest again, but I didn't wander . . . into the shadows' (*New Moon,* p341).

While Bella does live in a town surrounded by magnificent forest, a forest can have special meaning in a dream. Forests are wild places, untamed by humans, and so they offer escape from the demands of everyday life. Forests also stand for the wild and unknown territory of the unconscious mind. So wandering through a dark forest may be indicating that an important idea or worry is lurking at the back of a dreamer's mind.

Since Bella's dream involves visiting a forest, this may mean that her unconscious mind is trying to reveal a wild desire or an evolving fantasy, such as her 'hots' for Edward. Bella's forest is a 'shadowy' place, but not menacing. Therefore, the ideas trying to break through from Bella's unconscious mind to her conscious awareness are probably 'positive' rather than 'negative'.

## Wolves

There was a 'great russet wolf . . . gigantic, monstrous, bigger than a bear. The wolf stared intently at me, trying to convey something vital with his intelligent eyes. The black-brown, familiar eyes of Jacob Black' (*New Moon*, p292).

In Western culture, wolves tend to have evil meanings. The wolf in 'Little Red Riding Hood' is a symbol of evil and predatory behavior. In Native American culture, however, the wolf is a magnificent guide, teacher, and source of sacred wisdom – it has positive meanings. Since 'big bad wolf' ideas are missing in Bella's dream, her wolf is probably a sign of 'good medicine'. With its 'intelligent eyes', Bella's wild wolf is more of a messenger than a menace. In fact, this dream helps Bella to recall the Quileute wolf legend.

## Fire

> I was looking at a gray, barren field and smelling the thick scent of burning incense in the air. I was not alone . . . Scattered all around me were smoking heaps . . . I had no desire to see the faces of the vampires they had executed, half afraid that I might recognize someone in the smoldering pyres.
>
> (*Breaking Dawn*, p33)

The meaning of fire in a dream is complex and depends on other information inside the dream landscape. Fire can mean passion, the spirit, purification, transformation, illumination, anger or destruction. People can also get 'fired up' (excited) or 'burned' (hurt). In Bella's dream, the fire is destructive and she feels 'afraid'. Deep down, in Bella's unconscious, something in her waking life is a major threat to her (the Volturi, no doubt).

## Running

'No matter how fast I ran, I couldn't catch up with him' (*Twilight*, p58).

Running is a common dream theme that indicates a person's

need to escape or get away from someone or something that is too overwhelming. Or maybe the dreamer just needs to follow a slower pace of life. In Bella's dream, she is running *towards* something. This suggests that she wants to get up close and personal to something or someone. Since Bella has not yet 'caught up' with the subject of her dream, this suggests that she has a strong need that has not yet been fulfilled.

## Storms

'I dreamt I was outside in the storm, the wind whipping my hair in my face and blinding my eyes. I stood on the rocky crescent of First Beach' (*Eclipse*, p234).

Just before Bella had this dream, she heard a tale about human sacrifice. A chief's wife stabbed herself with a dagger to save her tribe from being slaughtered by a ruthless vampire. The storm in Bella's dream may be an unsettled unconscious response to this story. Storms in dreams can also point to rough challenges and ruffled emotional times in life. In Bella's dream, she does not seek 'shelter' from the storm. Instead, Bella is in the midst of it as the wind 'whips' at her hair. Perhaps this means that Bella is brave – she prefers to *face* her fears and problems rather than *hide* from them.

***

As you can see, Bella's dreams help to show that the unconscious mind is an infinite well of hidden psychological power. Bella's dreams reveal creative ideas and wise solutions. They reveal romantic desires and inner strength. Her dreams also suggest exciting possibilities to pursue – Edward, namely. If you want to figure out your own potential and possibilities – and unlock the power of your amazing unconscious – then, as Bella does in the Twilight epic, all you have to do is dream, dream, dream.

2

# I Sense: Intuitive Power in the Twilight Zone

*The intuitive mind is a sacred gift and the rational mind is a faithful servant. We have created a society that honors the servant and has forgotten the gift.*
- Albert Einstein, physicist

**Twilight's Mind-Readers**

The upside of being a supernatural creature in the Twilight Saga is having special powers. Edward, for example, is a highly gifted vampire who can read minds (except Bella's, of course). Edward first reveals his unusual secret to Bella in Port Angeles: 'I was . . . randomly searching through the thoughts of people on the street – to see if anyone had noticed you' (*Twilight*, p152–153).

In the Twilight world, there are others with extrasensory perception (ESP). Shape-shifting wolves have mind-reading powers too. All the wolves within a pack can read each other's thoughts simultaneously and they can communicate to each other in thoughts as a group – even across long distances. As Jacob explains: 'When we're wolves, we can . . . hear each other . . . not hear sounds . . . but we can hear *thoughts* – each other's' (*New Moon*, p317). Since wolves bond closely to each other, it makes sense that they have shared mind-reading powers so that they can hunt together and survive in the wild forest.

Although the human ability to read minds telepathically is an unresolved parapsychological matter, the Twilight books highlight another fascinating ability that relates closely to mind-reading power. It's the next best thing and it's called *intuition*. Where do you find the best intuitive action in the *Twilight* world?

Inside Bella's mind, mostly. It is a mysterious and mighty psychological gift.

## What Is Intuition?

Have you ever had a 'feeling' about something, but you're not exactly sure where that feeling came from? Well, that's probably intuition at work – your body sending you a special message. The *Penguin Dictionary of Psychology* defines intuition as 'a mode of understanding or knowing characterized as direct and immediate and occurring without conscious thought or judgement'. It is 'a response to subtle cues and relationships apprehended implicitly, unconsciously'. In other words, intuition means knowing something without really knowing how you know.

Another psychological view of intuition is that it is an ability to see things in terms of possibilities and future goals. An intuitive mind asks questions like: 'What might happen?' 'What is possible?' 'What does this situation suggest?' The implications of an experience are much more important to intuitives than the actual experience itself. Isabel Myers-Briggs, who developed a personality test to measure intuition based on the theories of Jung, says that people with intuitive tendencies like to:

- Mentally live in the future
- Be imaginative, create new possibilities
- Look for patterns, links, and meanings
- Use past information to make sense of the present and future

In the Twilight series, Bella's intuitive flair clearly keeps her ahead of the craziest predicaments. For example, vampires are supposed to be dangerous monsters designed with 'looks that kill'. But intuitive Bella sees more behind the predatory gleam in Edward's eyes. She senses emotional 'agony' behind his closed eyes (*Twilight*, p238), a gentle and tender nature (*New Moon*, p26), and above all, 'soul' (*Breaking Dawn*, p22). Bella shows she has a strong sense of intuition.

## The High Five

Imagine the sight of a brilliant Quileute bonfire blazing away at night, the warmth of its flames, the smell of its smoke, the sound of firewood crackling, and maybe the taste of wild vegetables baked in the burning hot coals. The human body has sensory receptors that receive and transmit these signals to the brain. In psychology, the study of 'sensation' and 'perception' is the biological basis for understanding intuition, such as Bella's. This area of psychology examines how organisms experience their environment.

*Sensation* is the initial contact between organisms and their physical surroundings. In particular, five key senses are used to register sensory stimuli: sight, sound, touch, taste, and smell. After the senses have detected and uploaded important information from the outside, they process it. *Perception* is how living creatures such as humans organize and interpret this information to achieve conscious experiences and make meaningful interpretations of their surroundings.

Just how good are your high five? Researcher Eugene Galanter found that the human body's five essential sensory receptors are so sensitive and powerful that they can detect the faintest of stimuli:

- Sight – on a clear night, the human eye can see a candle 30 miles away (that's 48 kilometers!).
- Sound – the ears can detect the ticking of a watch 20 feet away (6 meters).
- Taste – the tongue can taste a teaspoon of sugar dissolved in 2 gallons (7.5 liters) of water.
- Touch – a person can feel the wispy wing of a bee, barely

noticeable, fall on his or her cheek.
- Smell – a human can smell a single drop of perfume in a three-bedroom apartment.

In this Twilight meadow scene, Bella senses a cool flickering feeling at the end of her fingertip: 'I reached out one finger and stroked the back of his shimmering hand, where it lay within my reach. I marvelled again at the perfect texture, satin smooth, cool as stone' (*Twilight*, p229). Edward's skin feels cool and smooth to Bella as it sparkles, just like diamonds, in the sun.

As you can see, the five basic senses are pretty good at picking up and processing information from the outside world. This is why it is *sooo* important to have truckloads of orange blossom, lilac, freesia, and roses at your wedding – it would look and smell spectacular! And why your nose should steer clear of rotting tomatoes, wet werewolf hair, and sweaty socks and jocks. The pick-up power of the high five is what helps the intuitive sense come alive.

## Bella the Intuitive

In the Twilight world, Bella's intuition helps her to be happy, successful and safe. Since the first book of the series, Bella has always perceived and processed information in her world differently and perhaps a little more carefully than most other people. As Bella confirms: 'I wondered if I was seeing the same things through my eyes that the rest of the world was seeing in theirs' (*Twilight*, p9–10). As a result, a pattern of behavior that emerges in the novels is Bella's extra-sharp senses and intuitive abilities. In all four Twilight Saga books, Bella is adept at listening to her instincts, reading between the lines, noticing information under the surface, discovering hidden meanings, and foretelling potentially bad situations. The five senses pick up information; but the sixth sense – intuition – fills in the gaps: 'In the dead silence, all the details suddenly fell into place for me with a burst of intuition. Something Edward didn't want me to know . . . It was never going to end was, it?' (*Eclipse*, p71). In this important scene, Bella's intuition helps her to figure out that the villainous vampire Victoria will never stop hunting Bella until she kills her.

Another great example of Bella's intuitive prowess is that she correctly detects Edward's 'goodness' (using her sixth sense) behind the observable facts (the five senses): '"I can't explain it right . . . but he's even more unbelievable *behind* the face." The vampire who wanted to be good – who ran around saving people's lives so he wouldn't be a monster' (*Twilight*, p179).

Bella's intuitive sense about Edward's goodness leads her in a positive direction. In fact, a lecturer in the human potential movement, Stuart Wilde, wrote that: 'If a direction is right, you will know it automatically. If, however, making up your mind requires you to go through great trials and tribulations, you can be sure that particular course is not the one for you.' Thanks to Bella's intuition, she develops greater tolerance and compassion towards all good vampires and falls in love with her favorite one.

## Is There a Sixth Sense?

So how does Bella use her five senses (sensation) and interpret information (perception) to obtain hidden knowledge (intuition)? The human body is such as amazing tool that scientific studies are finding astonishing evidence to support the idea that there really *is* an intuitive 'sixth sense'. Recent research evidence suggests that in addition to the human body's 'five' basic senses, another superior sense exists. It's not Edward-like ESP or telepathic twittering among wolves. It's an invisible, sophisticated, and highly attentive sensory organ called the *immune system*.

## Riddled with Radars

According to the latest scientific theories, the immune system is much more than a mechanism that fights off disease. 'It is a specialised network of bio-sensors designed to pick up information from within and around the body and relay it to the brain, where it can motivate animals or people to behave in specific ways,' reports Rick Weiss on the subject. A loud growling noise, for example, will make people look around for danger. If the eyes detect ferns stirring in a dark forest, this will put people on alert. In the same way, the immune system is an intricate detection device 'riddled with radars' designed to detect a wide range of signals, which trigger adaptive behaviors.

In this important Twilight adventure, for example, Bella shows her uncanny ability to sense unseen activity in a dark classroom:

> As the room went black, I was suddenly hyperaware that Edward was sitting less than an inch from me. I was stunned by the unexpected electricity that flowed through me, amazed it was possible to be more aware of him than I already was. A crazy impulse to reach over and touch him . . . overwhelmed me.
> (*Twilight*, p191–192)

Bella cannot see, hear, smell, touch or taste Edward *directly*. But her ability to sense Edward *indirectly* and feel the 'electricity' between them makes sound sense according to immune system theory. A neuroscientist at the University of Colorado, Steven Maier, says that 'the immune system is essentially a sense organ'. It is 'spread around the body more than most senses are', he says. As Bella helps to show, intuition is like a game of 'I spy with my little "super-sensitive and very widespread" immune system'.

After picking up and processing important information, some simple behaviors that the highly sensitive immune system can trigger include hugging, huddling, shivering or sleeping – comfort-seeking actions that are sometimes mistaken as signs of illness or distress. Yet, our internal immune system 'knows' that these behaviors are incredibly beneficial. Some immune-prompted responses fight infection, prevent disease, or aid recovery. In this Twilight adventure, for example, Bella explains that: 'The flow of blood from my head sucked my consciousness away with it. My eyes were closing . . . and I drifted' (*Twilight*, p393). Bella faints after a vicious vampire injures her. Whether Bella's fainting is due to blood loss, broken bones, physical pain, or the mental shock of being attacked, one thing is for sure: Bella's body makes her 'faint'. This will reduce Bella's need to process environmental stimuli. As a result, her body can rest and recover more quickly.

## The 'Sex' Sense

Due to advances in molecular testing methods, scientists have discovered that the immune system talks to the brain – a lot. Researchers have been able to track tiny chemicals that the immune system secretes and have studied their effects on the central nervous system. A key research topic is 'sexual attraction'. It appears that the intuitive immune system tells people which person they should date and mate. One way the immune system influences how animals and people choose partners is by processing different scents, just as Edward does at his extra-powerful vampire level. 'Cupid, it seems, lives partly in a section of the immune system that varies a lot among individuals – and that gives animals scents that some can detect and unconsciously analyse,' reports Weiss in his article. Edward may be a vampire, but he illustrates the scent-sensing mating theory perfectly:

> The fragrance coming off your skin . . . I thought it would make me deranged that first day. In that one hour, I thought of a hundred different ways to lure you from the room with me, to get you alone . . . In that close, warm little room, the scent was maddening.
>
> (*Twilight*, p236–237)

To Edward's super sense of smell, Bella has an irresistible 'mouth-watering' and 'very floral smell, like lavender . . . or freesia' (*Twilight*, p267). This seems to drive his immune system crazy.

Some of the latest research evidence shows that people and animals really do use 'scents' to choose their mates and that the hot favorites are individuals who have *unlike* immune systems. Maybe this is a survival strategy to prevent inbreeding or to maintain genetic diversity. In one experiment, women sniffed T-shirts worn by various men and were asked which men they would like to date based on the smell. The girls almost always chose shirts worn by guys whose immune systems were most different to their own.

This immune system theory may explain why Edward loves Bella's scent so much. Smells processed by the immune system lead to love – as Bella's nose also shows: 'I smelled his cool breath in my face. Sweet, delicious, the scent made my mouth water. It was unlike anything else. Instinctively, unthinkingly, I leaned in closer, inhaling' (*Twilight*, p230). Just as strongly as Edward is drawn to Bella's scent (she is Edward's '*la tua cantante*' – her blood sings to him, says *New Moon*, p490), Bella is extremely 'intoxicated' by Edward's sweet scent too (*Twilight*, p249). When it comes to sexual attraction, the nose knows a lot. It definitely serves as a 'sexth' sense.

## Develop Your Intuitive Powers

### Inner Indicators

> '*I* don't know how to read minds – but sometimes it seems like you're trying to say goodbye when you're saying something else.' That was the best I could sum up the sensation of anguish that his words triggered in me.
>
> (*Twilight*, p184)

Maybe it's goosebumps. Maybe it's a sick feeling or a cold shiver down the spine. Or maybe, as Bella shows above, it's a strong sense of inner 'anguish'. These crucial and creepy sensations are her intuitive powers at work. By detecting signs of nervous system arousal, Bella increases her chances of making the best decisions and taking the best course of action. Whenever Bella needs to dodge danger, survive a crisis, escape an enemy or make a split-second choice to save someone she loves – and she is not sure what to do – she listens to her super-subtle internal signals to gauge situations on the spot.

Do you want your future to be successful and make fewer disappointing choices? If you know how to read the signs that suggest something is happening – like the intuitive Bella does – your next move may be your best one. Your next answer may be the right one. And your next decision may make the difference between complete success and total failure. The Twilight series points to a number of intuitive indicators that can guide people to safety and away from danger.

## Racing Heart

If you want to tap into the power of your sixth sense, as Bella does, a good intuitive indicator is your heart:

> 'You're dangerous?' I guessed, my pulse quickening as I intuitively realized the truth of my own words . . .
>
> 'But not bad.'
>
> (*Twilight*, p80)

Bella's 'quick pulse' is her intuitive sense in action (maybe her immune system is processing subtle information it has picked up). A racing heart is telling Bella that Edward can be dangerous, if necessary.

In most situations, a racing pulse can keep you out of harm's way. For example, by alerting you not to walk through a dark forest at night with a stranger. Or with someone you do know but with whom you feel uncomfortable. Your body is picking up information to keep you safe and processing that data much faster than your brain can.

The same physical reaction can also point to positive things. If your heart throbs, as Bella's does around Edward, this may be a sign that you have found your love-match. When Bella spots Edward in the school car park, for example, she nearly crashes her truck into the car behind her (*Twilight*, p44). Bella's near car-crash is a sign of her 'love' more than her 'clumsiness' on this occasion.

The body's reaction is much faster and more immediate than the speed at which the logical and higher brain processes information. So while Bella may not understand why the sight of Edward makes her swing her truck's gear in reverse, her body is screaming 'Hey! I like him! I want him! He excites me!' As Robert Graves puts it: 'Intuition is the supra-logic that cuts out all the routine processes of thought and leaps straight from the problem to the answer.' In other words, intuition knows what is good for you *now*.

## Suspicious Mind

Another intuitive indicator is a suspicious mind. The unconscious mind can quickly pick up small clues that our conscious brain may have not yet detected. As Bella illustrates in these important examples:

- 'I was consumed by the mystery Edward presented' (*Twilight*, p57).
- 'My head was so filled with Edward. I tried to concentrate on my feet, but he kept creeping back into my thoughts' (*Twilight*, p64).
- 'I couldn't get rid of the nagging suspicion that I was the reason he [Edward] wasn't there' (*Twilight*, p44).
- 'My head was spinning, trying to analyse every word Edward had spoken today. What did he mean?' (*Twilight*, p67).

The 'There's something about Edward' factor is something that Bella's intuitive sense clearly and correctly picks up on. For example, Bella's mind notices that Edward is super-fast, super-strong and that his skin feels cold. Or else, a slight change in someone's tone of voice, a fleeting glance from someone, or the reappearance of a past memory in the mind can trigger uneasy thoughts or make you mull over an issue all day, says David Myers, professor of psychology and author of *Intuition: Its Powers and Perils*. As the sample scenes above suggest, Bella isn't being paranoid; she has detected a piece of information that doesn't seem to fit and it is therefore far more likely to mean something. Bella's acute intuition helps her to unravel Edward's secret identity as a vampire.

### Stomach Pain

If you have been ignoring concerns or not acting on your hunches, the body will produce physical distress reactions. Stomach pain, cramps, nausea, or twisted knots may appear because this is your body's final attempt at drawing your attention to something important. Some situations certainly made Bella feel sickly strange:

- 'My stomach twisted' (*Twilight*, p67).
- 'My stomach was already full – of butterflies' (*Twilight*, p78).
- 'My stomach twisted uneasily' (*Twilight*, p372).
- 'I felt a spasm of unease in my stomach' (*New Moon*, p41).

In such cases, Bella's intuition is trying to tell her that a certain situation may be a threat or else it may have special meaning for her. It is a sign for her to take some sort of action. Intuition is not called 'gut instincts' for nothing.

## Dark Humor

There's a saying that 'the truth hides in every joke'. And if you start to make some dark ones, like Bella does at times, your mind is probably alerting you to some sort of trouble, or something else – indirectly. Gallows humor, a form of 'black humor' that emerges whenever people sense danger, is the body sending you a sign, says Gavin de Becker, a threat management expert. He wrote a well-known book called *The Gift of Fear*. In the Twilight Saga, for example, Bella questions Edward: '"Do you have multiple personality disorder?" I asked severely' (*Twilight*, p70).

Ha, ha. A funny joke *on* the surface. *Beyond* the surface, however, Bella's intuition is telling her that Edward's personality is 'more' complicated than he is letting on. When Edward keeps changing his mind about being friends with Bella, she accurately picks up on his inner conflict, even though she doesn't know what that conflict is yet (that deep down, Edward 'likes' Bella).

The serious point about jokes is that people like Bella don't make 'severe' jokes when they feel completely comfortable, in control, and at ease. A dark, negative remark – even if it's expressed light-heartedly – may end up being a call for help or a sign that you need to take extra care and maybe revise your strategies.

## Born to Spy

### Body-Talk

Another important source of information for intuition is body language. Body-talk conveys a person's underlying emotions and intentions, regardless of what a person is saying. More importantly, anyone can read body language, as Jacob tells Bella:

> 'How do you know me so well, Jacob? Sometimes it's like you can read *my* mind.'
>
> 'Naw. I just pay attention.'
>
> (*New Moon*, p321)

You don't have to be a mind-reader to understand people. You just have to be a good people-reader. That is, examine other people's *emotional expression* and *nonverbal communication* – their 'body-talk'.

One of the most useful body-talk signs to pick up is *incongruent* behavior. Sometimes people 'say' one thing but 'mean' another. Words do not always match the message, as Bella notices straight away when Edward is not his usual self:

> 'Come for a walk with me,' he suggested in an unemotional voice, taking my hand.
>
> I didn't answer. I couldn't think of a way to protest, but I instantly knew that I wanted to. I didn't like this. *This is bad, this is very bad,* the voice in my head repeated again and again. (*New Moon,* p67)

Bella picks up on Edward's cold, uninviting body signals behind his verbal invitation to go for a walk. She correctly detects the incongruent behavior between his spoken words and the cold way he speaks them. Nonverbal body language is how people express emotions. *The International Encyclopedia of Psychology* explains that emotions are crucial to survival. Facial expression, tone of voice, and body movements clearly communicate internal emotional experiences to others.

Altogether, there are three elements involved in communication:

- Body language (55%)
- Tone of voice (38%)
- Words (7%)

As you can see, words only communicate a tiny 7% of our message. In contrast, almost all information and meaning in a message – a whopping 93% – is communicated nonverbally by body language and tone of voice (total behavior minus words).

One of the most memorable examples of nonverbal emotional communication in the Twilight Saga would have to be when Bella and Edward first sit together at school in biology class. Not one word was uttered between them in that scene. Yet, it is one of the most emotionally tense and intense scenes between Bella and Edward in the whole Twilight series:

- Edward 'suddenly went rigid in his seat'
- He 'stared at me'
- His face was 'hostile, furious'
- His eyes were 'coal black'
- Edward expressed an 'antagonistic stare'
- His posture was 'leaning away from me'
- He sat on 'the extreme edge of his chair'
- He 'averted his face'
- Edward 'never relaxed his stiff position'
- His hand was 'clenched into a fist'
- He 'looked like he wasn't breathing'
- He was 'glaring down' again
- He raced 'out the door'

(*Twilight*, p20–21)

As Edward illustrates, someone who is not in the best mood can glare, stare, sit uncomfortably or tense their muscles. An individual's body language can communicate anger, dominance, passiveness, depression, intimacy or affection in an instant. Who knows? Maybe Edward showed enough 'bad' body vibes to scare off a whole gang of newborn vampires.

As psychology research learns more about body-talk, people will become even better at reading other people accurately and intuitively, just as the intuitive Bella does in Twilight. This will empower everyone to:

- Be safer around others
- Cooperate with each other
- Detect untruthful behavior in criminals
- Promote health, healing and well-being

## Eye-Talk

An important form of communication in the Twilight books is eye contact. Eye-talk is a leading form of nonverbal communication between Bella and Edward. Interesting and expressive, the eyes provide considerable information for people to process. In the hospital scene below, Bella's intuition detects extra and important information that another's eyes cannot hide: '"Oh, well, yes," Dr. Cullen agreed, suddenly occupied with the papers in front of him. Then he looked away, at Tyler, and walked to the next bed. My intuition flickered; the doctor was in on it' (*Twilight*, p54).

When Bella tries to explain something to Dr Cullen, she notices that he averts his gaze and looks away from her when talking. This invokes Bella's intuition – her ability to 'read between the lines' – because she notices something 'odd' about his eye-talk. Uneasy eye action can convey a lot of emotional information like love, anger, fear or sadness or that something is wrong.

How informative is eye-talk as far as Bella and Edward are concerned? Very informative, according to Calin Prodan, a neurology professor at the University of Oklahoma. He says that it is worth paying particular attention to the upper part of the face. This is because false 'social emotions' tend to be expressed on the lower half of the face, while a person's real 'primary emotions' leak out across the upper half, mostly around the eyes. Here are a few compelling eye-talk scenes from book one:

- '"Will you do something for me this weekend?" He turned to look me straight in the face, utilizing the full power of his burning gold eyes. I nodded helplessly' (*Twilight*, p93). It's not the verbal command that convinces Bella to do Edward a favor. It's the direct eye-contact and those 'burning gold' eyes that do the talking.

- 'I saw how light his eyes were, lighter than I'd ever seen them, golden butterscotch. "I feel very safe with you," I confessed' (*Twilight*, p148). Something bright and warm about Edward's eyes helps Bella to feel safe and secure in his company. As a matter of fact, when people really like someone or something, their eyes open more widely.
- 'His lovely eyes seem to glow with rash excitement' (*Twilight*, p232). Exactly. Studies show that when people are really happy or excited, their pupils dilate. This, in turn, elicits positive reactions from others.

The eyes are our most expressive feature. Eyes are gateways to information and windows to the soul. In particular, our attentive intuition finds eye-talk useful and informative. Meanwhile, the emotions that accompany eye-talk can be so intense and powerful that anyone can dazzle others with their eyes.

### Crim-Talk: Volturi Vibes

Anyone is capable of criminal thoughts and violent actions. However, some individuals are regularly violent or are much more likely to be violent than others – selfish vampires, cruel Volturi guards, human aggressors. As many people would already know and psychological research confirms, dangerous individuals show 'signs' of potential violence beforehand. To protect yourself from violence, one of the best psychology tricks is to use your attention and intuition for spotting any 'pre-incident indicators'. In other words, look for verbal and nonverbal clues that suggest a certain person is likely to harm others. Gavin De Becker is a leading authority in the field of threat assessment and the prediction and management of violence. He worked his whole life to formularize the violent mindset so that others could also see the signs – and save people's lives from violence. He says that 'you can know when you are in the presence of danger. You have the gift of a brilliant internal guardian that stands ready to warn you of hazards and guide you through risky situations'. In the Twilight world, the Volturi leader Aro shows that some warning signs are truly weird:

> 'Alice and Bella!' he rejoiced, clapping his thin hands together. 'This *is* a happy surprise! Wonderful!' I stared in shock as he called our names informally, as if we were old friends dropping in for an unexpected visit.
>
> (*New Moon*, p467)

Bella's attention to body language and her intuitive interpretation of Aro's over-the-top charm and shallow sincerity accurately detects a violence indicator. While someone's false sweetness may not mean much on the surface, in reality it can be a sign of a disturbed and dangerous personality.

The British psychologist Dr Robert Hare is famous for his work on *psychopaths*. These are violence-prone individuals who are selfish, manipulative, impulsive and cold-hearted, much like the cunning and calculating Aro seems to be. What's more, the first item in Hare's test for determining if someone has a psychopathic streak is 'superficial charm' – Aro's nutcase quality in a nutshell. According to Dr Hare, this psychopathic feature points to:

> A shallow person who shows an insincere and superficial charm. He is often a clever and amusing speaker, but is too slick and smooth to be believed. He comes across as overly confident and claims to have expert knowledge about many things, but careful questioning reveals he is a fake. Although

he appears friendly and straightforward, he provides little useful information and tries to control the conversation.

This surely sounds like Aro and his sick, slick, and super-slimy style of crim-talk, don't you think? Aro is way too nice and far too friendly towards Bella, Edward and Alice in his ghoulish underground chambers. Consider these strange and superficially charming behaviors in front of guests whom Aro plans to kill in *New Moon*:

- Aro kisses Jane (one of his deadliest guards) and calls her 'a comfort' (p467) in front of Bella, Edward, and Alice whom he wants to murder later. What a weirdo.
- Although Aro talks about murdering Edward and Bella in front of everyone, he calls Jane his 'dear one' in a soft, sighing voice at the same time (p466). Bit bizarre, don't you think?
- Aro 'croons' (p469) and sings in a 'feathery voice' (p470) as he interrogates his hostages.
- Aro asks Bella if he can touch her hand, but Bella has already tuned in to his psychopathic behavior: 'Despite Aro's overt politeness, I didn't believe I had a choice' (p473). In line with Dr Hare's research, Bella accurately detects an 'insincere' and 'controlling' psychopath.

As a psychologist who has worked with many violent offenders in prison and in the community, I know that violence is a pattern of behavior that is riddled with special clues. Although predatory criminals try to present themselves as 'normal' individuals, violent people just can't hide their psychopathic streak. Their odd crim-talk oozes through:

- They're *too* nice
- They talk too much

- They like to insult people, to deliberately provoke a reaction
- They're not shocked about things that upset many other people
- They're excessively calm
- They need to control conversations and situations all the time
- They boast too much

(Source: Hare; De Becker)

When it comes to baby-faced 'Jane', for example, the Volturi's very own terminator, what's there not to shudder about? This Volturi vixen is the epitome of a cruel, ruthless sadist – not the best person to invite over for your Saturday night pajama party. What crim-talk clues does the Volturi's weapon of pain reveal?

> Jane turned toward us with a beatific smile.
> Before I could react . . . Edward was on the ground.
> No one had touched him, but he was on the stone floor writhing in obvious agony, while I stared in horror.
> Jane was smiling only at him now.
> (*New Moon*, p474–475)

In this scene, Bella's reaction is one of instant 'horror', which is a normal reaction. She feels *empathy* for Edward who is in extreme physical pain. In stark psychological contrast, Jane's 'smiles' are *callous* (lacking in empathy) and way off normal. Cruel and callous behavior is a core feature of the psychopath. By listening to your intuition, reading people, and watching for crim-talk clues such as people laughing at other people's suffering, or other unsound emotional reactions, you can become skilled at picking up these kinds of Volturi vibes.

According to behavior experts, attentive intuition is an excellent and reliable source of safety and protection. Crime reports show that many victims of attacks already 'knew' that something didn't 'feel quite right' about a certain something or someone, just before an attack occurred. So to protect yourself from violence, as the Twilight Saga suggests, the trick is to trust your intuition and avoid people and places that are *not* comfortable, whenever and wherever you can. Using your 'gift' of fear, your inner intuition, and reading people for crim-talk can save your life.

## A Znakharka Knows

In wild and wintery East Europe, where the fearful vampire legends arose, intuitive knowledge has been revered and relied upon since the earliest times. An accepted way to access superior intuitive wisdom to this day is to talk to a *znakharka* – the 'all-knowing one' – for information, guidance and healing. These wise female folk healers from Ukraine perform meditative magic rituals, remove maladies and help people to cope better with life. They brew medicine, interpret dreams, cast spells, detect poisons, identify enemies, and will even repel the Evil Eye. Just as precognitive Alice does in the Twilight adventures, a znakharka might even read your past, present, and future. I guess intuition is extra-handy when you live in vampire country.

Next time you feel stuck or scared, you're not sure what to do or decide, and you don't have access to a mind-reading vampire or a telepathic werewolf, why not free your inner znakharka:

- Tune in to your intuition
- Listen to your inner voice
- Take note of your heart, gut or other strange sensations
- Hone in on the hunch
- Acknowledge uneasy feelings or unusual information

As many exciting adventures from the Twilight Saga show, your intuition is a powerful sixth sense.

# 3

# I Love: The Relentless Hunt for Affection

*With love's light wings did I o'er-perch these walls;*
*For stony limits cannot hold love out,*
*And what love can do that dares love attempt.*
- William Shakespeare, *Romeo and Juliet*

## We Burn to Bond

Romance. Friendship. Marriage. Family. Community. All these relationships evolve in the Twilight Saga. Why? A burning desire to bond with others. As Edward admits to Bella: 'I should leave now. But I don't know if I can . . . I crave your company too much' (*Twilight*, p223). Since love is central to human happiness and is a main theme in the Twilight books, it makes you wonder just how well our favorite vampires, werewolves and humans are bonding with each other. There's no doubt about it. Love is the most powerful drug of all and the ultimate brand of heroin. Love it or hate it, we are all restless and relentless hunters of love.

## True Love: Bella and Edward

The big psychological theme of the Twilight books is *love*. This fantasy series is basically a romantic tale about an unexpected and forbidden love between Bella (a human) and Edward (a vampire). But what is love? Is it a scientific psychological concept? Or just a load of mushy nonsense? From a psychological point of view, what kind of love do Bella and Edward experience, anyway? How closely bonded are they? A recent view in social psychology suggests that there are many different kinds of love. 'Love can be many different things, depending in large part on the nature of the relationship. The love you feel for your parents is different to the love you feel for your romantic partner. All of these varieties of love differ,' says psychologist Steven Breckler.

### What Is Love?

According to the *International Encyclopedia of Psychology,* love is defined as a mixture of three crucial ingredients: passion, intimacy, and commitment.

- Passion – an intense desire to be with another person. It is expressed through hugging, kissing, and sexual behavior.
- Intimacy – a feeling of emotional closeness and connectedness, expressed through communication, interaction and doing things to support the other person.
- Commitment – a decision to love another person and then taking action to maintain and protect that love over time. It is often expressed as devotion and loyalty.

The 'amount' of love one feels for someone depends on the *strength* of each component. In comparison, the 'kind' of love one feels for another depends on the *mixture* of these components. So what is Bella and Edward's romantic recipe?

### It's Passionate

From the very beginning, Bella and Edward's love for each other is very *passionate*. In the Twilight world, vampires call this intense love '*La tua cantante*' (*New Moon,* p490), werewolves call it 'imprinting' (*Eclipse,* p109), and humans use the phrase 'love-at-first-sight' (*Eclipse,* p111). Passionate love is a strong and sudden feeling of 'falling into love'. It starts off as a compelling emotional fascination or sexual attraction towards another person without the intimacy and commitment components. It involves a great longing to be with the person of your heart's desire. Reciprocated love (when people are united with each other) produces strong feelings of fulfillment and euphoria. Meanwhile, unrequited love (when people are separated from their loved ones and cannot receive another's love) produces strong feelings of emptiness, anxiety, or despair.

In the Twilight books, Bella and Edward's love for each other illustrates psychology's view of passionate love. When Bella and Edward first saw each other, it was love at first sight – an instant and powerful attraction to each other. The first time Bella ever saw Edward she described him as 'the beautiful boy' (*Twilight*, p17). And the first time Edward saw Bella, well before he had a chance to sniff her special scent, he gazed at her with 'evident curiosity in his expression' and an 'unmet expectation' (*Twilight*, p19). A good example of Bella's initial fascination with Edward is when she thinks to herself: 'I was consumed by the mystery Edward presented. And more than a little obsessed' (*Twilight*, p57). At the same time, Edward's curiosity was just as powerful. He admits to Bella: 'You're not like anyone I've ever known. You fascinate me' (*Twilight*, p214).

When couples like Bella and Edward love each other passionately, they engage in behavior called *perceptual accentuation*. That's when partners idealize each other and only see each other's positive features. Some people refer to this romantic phenomenon as 'love is blind'. In the Twilight world, for example, Bella often describes Edward as 'perfect' (*Twilight*, p224) and fully reassures him that 'It doesn't matter to me what you are' (*Twilight*, p161). At the same time, Edward idealizes Bella. To him, she looks beautiful whether she's wearing clothes with 'holes' in them or her hair sticks up like a 'haystack' (*Twilight*, p261, p273). Beauty is in the eyes of the love-affected beholder. The more partners believe their idealistic illusions, the more intense the passion between them. Passion sets love on fire. As Bella and Edward show, people are passionately in love when they always think about the other person, hunger to be with the other person, and feel ecstatic when in the company of their love-interest. Although Edward is a vampire who wants to drink Bella's blood, she confesses in this famous *Twilight* quote: 'I was unconditionally and irrevocably in love with him' (p171).

## It's Intimate

If Bella and Edward's love is true, it must involve more than just passion. The second crucial ingredient of love is *intimacy*. At the core of all close relationships is 'intimacy – an interactive process in which a person feels understood, validated, and cared for as the result of a partner's response,' says social psychology expert Dr Breckler. It is intimacy that securely attached people achieve in their close relationships. A process of self-disclosure is essential for developing intimate relationships in which partners understand and support each other's needs and interests. This seems to happen in Bella and Edward's relationship.

As the love between Bella and Edward evolves, the first critical incident of self-disclosure occurs on an unplanned date in Port Angeles. In a private corner of a local restaurant, Edward tells Bella about his mind-reading powers and warns her that he is 'dangerous'. This clue helps Bella to figure out that he really is a vampire (*Twilight*, p148–160). An honest exchange of personal information builds up trust and helps people to learn about each other accurately. This promotes feelings of emotional closeness in relationships. Activities like self-disclosure, responding appropriately to another person's needs, and showing empathy achieve the intimacy component of true love.

Steadily but surely, the Twilight books show that Bella, who is usually a shy, private and reserved person, grows more trusting, talkative, and comfortable around Edward. For example, Bella clearly feels contented when she thinks to herself: 'his quiet, probing questions kept me talking freely, forgetting, in the dim light of the storm, to be embarrassed' (*Twilight*, p203). Edward's genuine interest in Bella and his responsive listening skills draw her out of her shell. Of course, Edward self-discloses more about himself too, which strengthens his emotional bond with Bella and provides further evidence of an intimate love: 'Having you know about everything, not needing to keep secrets from you . . . I *like* it. It makes me happy' (*Twilight*, p300). As self-disclosure evolves, the intimate love between Bella and Edward grows stronger. Over time, as a couple continues to disclose thoughts and feelings to one another, this helps partners to develop a really 'intimate' understanding of how to look after each other. When you get to know another person thoroughly and intimately, you also increase your chances of achieving a happy long-term relationship and making love last.

## It's Committed

So far, according to the psychological approach to love, Bella and Edward show true love in that they connect to each other passionately and intimately. But the third component of healthy love is *commitment*. Are Bella and Edward committed to each other? In all four books of the Twilight series, Bella and Edward sure do provide some pretty powerful examples of a committed love. When Bella says to Edward: 'You *are* my life. You're the only thing it would hurt me to lose' (*Twilight*, p413), she admits she has bonded exclusively with Edward and is willing to commit herself fully to their relationship.

Other powerful examples of Bella and Edward's commitment to each other:

- Bella is willing to become a vampire so she can stay with Edward (*Twilight*, p413).
- Edward asks Bella to marry him (*New Moon*, p540).
- Bella and Edward go to extraordinary lengths to protect each other (e.g. *Eclipse*, p488, p490).
- Bella is prepared to live in Antarctica and eat penguins if

she has to (*Eclipse,* p23).

- Bella does everything in her power to protect Edward and his family (*Twilight,* p371, p375, p377; *Eclipse,* p416–417, p478).

Maybe the most romantic example of Bella and Edward showing commitment to their relationship is when they pledge eternal loyalty, with their lives, to each other. Bella makes this powerful promise to Edward: 'I'd rather die than be with anyone but you' (*New Moon,* p45). Likewise, Edward makes a similar vow to Bella: 'Bella, I can't live in a world where you don't exist' (*New Moon,* p509). When romantic rapport involves passion, intimacy and commitment as suggested in Bella and Edward's relationship, this is a sure-fire sign of true love.

## Romance: Twilight's Twist

### The Love Game

In the game of love, Bella and Edward are definite winners and arguably Twilight's favorite couple. Romantically, Bella and Edward get together and stay together as a passionate, intimate and committed duo. In fact, Edward and Bella have bonded together so closely that even Marcus, a Volturi leader and people-eater who has the power to read relationships, was 'surprised at the intensity' of their union (*New Moon,* p471). Bella and Edward seem to make a perfect pair. Well then, where does this leave Jacob? He also loves Bella passionately, knows her intimately, and is committed to looking after her. Dumped for a blood-sucker, it looks like happy and sunny Jacob has been left to howl and prowl all alone in the cold snow. He didn't get the girl of his dreams, the love of his life – Bella. This surely makes Jacob a loser in the cruel game of love. Er, does it?

Twilight reveals a romantic twist that is a shocker for more reasons than what prowls on the surface. To start with, the result that Jacob did not win the 'obvious' prize (Bella) is really a mixed blessing in disguise. It makes Jake a winner in the end because he did not end up with someone who does not love him in the way he desires. But wait, there's more. As you will now see, Twilight's romantic twist appears to contain several other symbolic and supernatural signs that might give Jacob first place in the crazy game of love. And these clues are more twisted than the original twister.

## A Surprise Match

The obvious twist that Jacob wins the game of love is that he 'imprints' on Renesmee (Bella's baby daughter, who will reach adulthood in just a few years). 'Nessie', as Jacob affectionately calls her, adores Jacob fully in return. Yes, semi-supernatural Ness is hells-bells in love with Jake.

Most importantly, Renesmee is no consolation prize. On the contrary, Jacob may have fallen in love with the most powerful character in the Twilight series as these neat Nessie 'power' clues suggest:

### Power clue # 1: super-*duper* compassion

Jacob falls in love with a girl who shows super-powerful compassion. Everything Renesmee touches, she charms and calms. While her mother Bella uses a supernatural 'shield' to project care *around* others, Renesmee's gift is far greater. She has the ability to compel others *to* care. Those who have been 'touched' by Renesmee's gift convince and inspire others to care also. In *Twilight and Philosophy*, Andrew and Jenny Terjesen agree that Renesmee 'cements Carlisle's alliance of witnesses to stand with him against the Volturi . . . She creates connections almost immediately with . . . others. Those connections make them want to take care of her'.

Renesmee's ability to quell destructive desires, create loving relationships with everyone around her, and encourage others to care is a form of super-*duper* compassion with unlimited potential. With a mother who cares about others (Bella), a grandfather who is super-compassionate (Carlisle), and the possession of a 'natural' gift to encourage care that will be 'nurtured' in a caring Cullen environment, this half-vampire babe is a pretty powerful weapon of love. But wait, there's more.

**Power clue # 2: two forces**

Another clue to support the view that Jacob is a big relationship winner is Renesmee's *dual* nature. Renesmee is both a human *and* a vampire. She inherits the best of both sides and combines characteristics from both worlds. As two traditional enemies (humans and vampires) merge into one, Renesmee rises above the usual prejudices that divide races and species. Not only is Renesmee a 'magnet for care', she is powerful proof that two opposite and repelling forces can exist peacefully together.

According to an official sourceon the meaning of numbers, the number two denotes division and conflict but also balance and synchronicity. In support of this, Renesmee's binary nature harmoniously embraces the positive and negative aspects of all things – day/night, light/dark, good/bad, love/hate and life/death. Renesmee therefore symbolizes harmonious love. Even the name Renesmee (which joins the human name 'Renee' together with the vampire name 'Esme') is a gesture to such harmony. This makes Nessie a doubly powerful partner for Jake. But wait, there's more.

**Power clue # 3: three forces**

When you think about it, Renesmee embraces three different life forces. You see, Nessie has 1) a human mother, 2) a vampire father *and* 3) a supernatural link with her shape-shifting husband-to-be Jacob because he *imprints* on her. So Renesmee fuses three species into one (human + vampire + shape-shifter). She is three disparate fates woven together into a single thread.

As a result, Renesmee has links with the number 'three – the first true magical number'. The number three is often seen as the number of wisdom, understanding and spiritual knowledge – as in the Holy Trinity, the Buddhist's Triple Jewel and the three directions of magic (past, present, future). 'There's a sense of satisfaction and pattern about threes as in "third time lucky",' writes symbol expert Adele Nozedar. But wait, there's more.

### Power clue # 4: the fourth force

Renesmee also has links to the number four. Why? Because Renesmee is the *fourth* individual who enters and ends the long game of love. Since Renesmee is Jacob's magical match and future mate, she finally puts to rest the ever-struggling love triangle between Bella, Edward and Jacob that has caused the trio so much angst. As a result, Renesmee balances the power of three.

In fact, the number four traditionally symbolizes harmony and balance. The *Element Encyclopedia of Secret Signs and Symbols* explains that a square's four sides are 'protective and stable' and 'hold things box-like within the embrace of its confines'. There are four natural elements in magic and astrology – air, water, earth, and fire. In alchemy, four key ingredients make the Philosopher's Stone – sulphur, mercury, salt, and azoth. Other patterns of four include the four seasons and the four suits in playing cards. This makes Bella's immediate family of four (Bella + Edward + Jake + Nessie) a powerful quadratic love formula indeed.

## Twilight's Powerful Pair

In light of the above 'power clues', a love alliance between Jacob and Renesmee may make them the most powerful couple of all in the Twilight epic. But wait, there's just a bit more. Consider Jacob – he believes in freedom, democracy, justice, and is a powerful leader. His soul-mate and future bride Renesmee promotes love, peace, care and therefore hope (and she's still just an infant). Just imagine the unlimited power that these two open-minded and open-hearted individuals can wield in a world to make it better, free of hate and harm. Jacob and Renesmee are a romantic success, an incredible influence, and probably Twilight's most powerful supernatural pair.

### Best Friends: Bella and Jacob

In addition to romantic relationships, the Twilight world values other important relationships. Above all, *friendship*. From assorted associates at Bella's school to loyal links among orphaned vampires to camaraderie among Quileute wolves, friendship underscores all important relationships and is an important psychological theme in the Twilight novels. Who has the strongest and most gossiped-about friendship in the Twilight Saga? Who else but Bella and Jacob:

> 'We're a pretty messed up pair, aren't we?' Jacob said . . .
>
> 'Pathetic,' I agreed . . .
>
> 'At least we have each other,' he said, clearly comforted by the thought.
>
> I was comforted, too. 'At least there's that,' I agreed.
>
> (*New Moon*, p349)

Although Bella loves Edward romantically, she is closely connected with Jacob as a friend. No matter how messed up you think you are, there's always room in your heart for others who think they're messed up too.

Why is it that Bella, Edward, Jacob – and everyone else on the planet – need friends? Why is there such a strong desire to go friendship hunting?

### Friendship Hunting

In psychology, friendship is also known as *companionate love*. Friendship is built on attraction (how much we like others), intimacy (emotional familiarity with each other) and affiliation (a natural desire to seek company). According to social psychology, our natural need to affiliate with others is what drives us to hunt down companionate love. The best friendships occur when certain factors are involved. These psychological friendship factors may help to explain just why Bella and Jacob have such a strong and enduring friendship.

### Propinquity

This is the geographical proximity or nearness of other people to you. People are more likely to form strong friendships with people who live close by. In their Twilight world, Bella and Jacob live near each other, just a short truck drive (or wolf sprint) down the road. This factor significantly increases the chances of developing a firm friendship.

### Physical attractiveness

People prefer to bond with individuals who they believe look attractive. This is because people associate physical attractiveness with other positive psychological qualities such as friendliness, courage and intelligence. Bella and Jacob are both physically fit and healthy individuals, who do look attractive in each other's eyes. Bella has definitely noticed Jacob's tanned and athletic physique and his strong and graceful movements. And Bella must be beautiful in Jacob's eyes because as soon as she turns into a vampire Jake tells her 'Bells. You're a freak show' (*Breaking Dawn*, p401).

### Similarity

Another important friendship factor is similarity. Good friends share common interests and goals. Similar values and commitments help to build trust between people. Over time, the friendship grows stronger. Bella and Jacob have very similar backgrounds. They both come from non-wealthy one-parent families, have career-driven dads ('chiefs'), and help to look after their family. A common background experience would definitely have encouraged Bella and Jacob to develop similar psychological qualities, attitudes and values. For example, both Bella and Jacob tend to be adventurous, independent, strong-willed and fiercely protective.

## Complementarity

An interesting friendship factor is that people who have *complementary* traits tend to form the closest and strongest friendship bonds. And in the Twilight books, Jacob and Bella are clearly complements – they are the Twilight Saga's sun and moon. In fact, a lot of information suggests that Bella and Jacob supplement each other well.

Bella's personality style is:

- Introverted: shy, private, not talkative (*Twilight*, p5)
- Apprehensive about expressing emotions (*Twilight*, p7)
- Not good at relating to people (*Twilight*, p9)
- Not interested in fashion, dancing, or dating lots of boys (*Eclipse*, p321)
- Not a party-goer (*Eclipse*, p321)
- Dreamy, intellectual and scholarly (e.g. she likes to discuss theories, read books)

Jacob's character is:

- Extraverted: lively, friendly, self-confident (*Twilight*, p103)
- Expressed through happy nonverbal communication (*Twilight*, p104; *New Moon*, p145)
- Open, honest, warm (*Twilight*, p104)
- Direct (*Twilight*, p109)
- Adventurous, optimistic, confident (*New Moon*, 196, p210, p212)

- Practical and mechanical (e.g. he likes to fix cars, carve wooden trinkets)

When Bella teams up with Edward as a partner, she never excludes Jacob as her friend. Both Team Edward (romance) and Team Jacob (friendship) are winners in their own special ways. Bella and Edward may be 'soul-mates' but Bella and Jacob are 'kindred spirits' (*Eclipse*, p64). Both teams involve affiliation and an intimate connection. Even though Edward (vampire) and Jacob (shape-shifting wolf) are traditional enemies, Bella strives to affiliate with everyone.

A companionate love that involves several friendship factors (like Bella and Jacob's friendship) is an unbeatable friendship, which would explain why Bella and Jacob like each other so much. In fact, researcher Zick Rubin (who developed a scale to measure how much people love and like each other) found that the best predictor of long-term relationships was not how much people *loved* each other but how much people *liked* each other. To 'like' someone is psychology's best-ever secret to any great relationship. Just as true love is a powerful force, a true friendship is just as formidable., Even vampires like Edward eventually understand and appreciate the indestructible friendship that Bella and Jacob share: 'When I left you, Bella, I left you bleeding. Jacob was the one to stitch you back up again. That was bound to leave its mark – on both of you' (*Eclipse*, p473).

Bells and Jake are the best of friends. They have forged an awesome bond with each other that is likely to last the distance.

## I Shield: Bella's Best Emo-Skill

In the Twilight Saga, Bella has a 'glitch' inside her brain that shields her from negative and intrusive mental energy. In fact, Bella's shield happens to be a unique and superlative quality of her psychological make-up. As Twilight fans know, it first comes to attention when Edward reveals his inability to read Bella's mind: 'It's harder than it should be – keeping track of you' (*Twilight*, p152) he tells her at Port Angeles. As the Twilight plot progresses, some important psychological information that emerges is that Bella's glitch may be her top emotional skill, helping her to boost her bonds with others.

## Mental Defense Mechanism?

At first, Bella's mental shield appears to be some kind of *mental defense mechanism*. This psychological idea was introduced by Dr Sigmund Freud in 1894. According to psychodynamic theory, the mind develops defenses to guard against unconscious conflicts. If a person feels any internal anxiety this motivates 'the ego to resort to defensive measures . . . to save it from experiencing pain,' says Anna Freud, who summarized her father's work. The main goal of ego defense mechanisms is to minimize problems, reduce anxiety, and protect the conscious mind from pain. Without a doubt, Bella's mental mechanism is exactly that:

> Some strange glitch in my brain . . . made it immune to all the extraordinary and frightening things some immortals could do . . . I was seriously grateful to whatever malfunction it was that kept my thoughts a secret.
>
> (*Breaking Dawn*, p22)

When a wise vampire named Eleazor meets Bella and notices that her mind is immune and impenetrable to the psychic probing and manipulation of other vampires, he calls her ability a 'shield' (*Breaking Dawn*, p552). This, in turn, leads another vampire, Kate, to ask if Bella can 'project' her protective ability – to shield others (*Breaking Dawn*, p555). As the Twilight Saga story evolves, it becomes more and more apparent that Bella's shield is not just a primitive defense mechanism that functions in an unconscious, automatic, and reactive way to decrease anxiety. Bella's mental shield is so much more.

## Empathy Action

As the final novel *Breaking Dawn* confirms, Bella's shield does not just work to reduce her own anxiety. Bella's shield also responds with care to her surroundings and protects others. It appears that Bella's shield develops into a conscious, deliberate, useful and proactive coping strategy. Namely, an important 'empathy' action of some kind. In psychology, empathy is defined as 'the awareness and understanding of the emotions and feelings of another person'. Empathy involves 'taking on the perspective of the person' as well as showing a 'vicarious affective response to the emotional experiences of another person,' says the *Penguin Dictionary of Psychology*. In other words, empathy means *understanding* and *responding* appropriately to other people's feelings. Consider Bella's expressions of empathy when she is still a human:

- Bella puts other people's happiness first (*Twilight*, p4).
- Bella thinks ahead as to how others might feel: 'I can't bear it if anyone has to be hurt because of me' (*Twilight*, p377).
- The slaughter of human tourists deep beneath the city of Volterra deeply distresses Bella (*New Moon*, p487).
- When Bella notices that Jacob looks as if he will cry, she comforts him with a big hug (*New Moon*, p178).
- Bella is very concerned about Jacob's emotional pain (*Eclipse*, p4).
- Bella feels upset when reading about a murder spree in Seattle as she examines life from the victims' point of view (*Eclipse*, p22).
- Bella's plan to be a vampire definitely excludes killing people (*Eclipse*, p23).

- Bella relates to Jacob's anguish and visualizes Jacob's face 'in pain' (*Eclipse*, p34).
- When facing evil vampires, Bella puts everyone else's safety first (*Twilight*, p342, 371, 375; *Eclipse*, p373).

As you can see, Edward may have a talent for reading people's minds but Bella can read people's emotions. Since Bella can adapt, regulate, and channel her protective instincts to care for others – 'flex her shield' so to speak – her glitch is more like an 'empathy action' rather than a simple 'defensive reflex'.

Most importantly, Bella's shield increases her power to form positive and productive relationships with others. If you want to bond with anyone else on the face of this planet, you cannot do so without empathy. It is the top factor of 'emotional intelligence' – the ability to monitor mood, manage emotions, and care about others, says psychologist Dr Daniel Goleman. For example:

- Bella spends time with her father to cheer him up: 'I watched TV with Charlie . . . It felt good, despite my depression, to make him happy' (*Twilight*, p129). Bella's empathy helps her to feel close to her dad.
- 'I vowed to myself that I would be in a good mood tonight and not ruin Angela's or Jessica's enjoyment in their dress hunting' (*Twilight*, p130). Not only does Bella care about the feelings of her friends, her considerate efforts will promote a positive atmosphere for all.
- 'His face startled me – his expression was torn, almost pained, and so fiercely beautiful' (*Twilight*, p192–193). Bella detects Edward's inner pain, which will surely help her to plan an appropriate emotional response and increase her emotional intimacy with him.
- '"You just walked in," Bella said. "After running all day, I'd bet. Put your feet up for a minute. I'll probably warm up again in no time"' (*Breaking Dawn*, p268). Although Bella feels

> cold and unwell, her heightened sensitivity to other people's feelings enables her to reach out and relate to others.

Bella's sophisticated psychological shield protects her from emotional pain, protects others from pain, and promotes her bonds with others.

Bella's empathy is especially evident when she declines to reveal her own worries in order to shield others from pain. For example, Bella does not want Jacob to worry about her nightmares, so she doesn't tell him about them: 'Jacob didn't need to have my nightmares' (*Eclipse*, p93). Some Twilight critics consider this behavior to be that of a deceitful 'liar' – behavior which makes Bella a dishonest and unlikeable character. However, Bella's reaction is empathy in action – a conscious and sophisticated emotional skill. One of the most famous teenage girls in the world did exactly the same things as Bella, just to protect those she truly loved from unnecessary worry: 'I soothe my conscience now with the thought that it is better for hard words to be on paper than that Mummy should carry them in her heart.' These are the celebrated words of Anne Frank, a Jewish teenage girl and a 20th-century heroine who kept a personal diary during World War Two. Still a teen, Anne died in a horrendous Nazi concentration camp. But her emo-genius lives on. The actions of both Bella and Anne suggest powerful emotional empathy, rather than thoughtless, antisocial or manipulative behavior.

In *Breaking Dawn*, Bella's shield becomes mighty powerful once she becomes a vampire. Her empathy develops into a psychic force field that she projects to protect others. With guidance and training from good vampires, Bella learns to extend her elastic shield, a 'strange reddish . . . spectrum of light . . . tainted with crimson' (*Breaking Dawn*, p575–576). Bella's best emo-skill empowers her to protect her precious relationships with others.

## Family Fever

## Loneliness Kills: Carlisle's Company

A world without love, affection, and company is a bare and barren place indeed. This was Dr Carlisle Cullen's world for a very long time, just after he changed into a vampire – desolate, deserted, lonely. Much later, when Carlisle encountered humans on the brink of mortal death, individuals without family, he turned them into immortal vampires. Since people such as Edward and Esme were already dying, Carlisle gave them supernatural life and subsequently created companions for himself. As Edward explains to Bella, Carlisle 'acted from loneliness. That's usually the reason behind the choice. I was the first in Carlisle's family, though he found Esme soon after. She fell from a cliff' (*Twilight*, p252). One can understand Carlisle's choice. Extreme or unwarranted loneliness is a highly painful and intolerable experience. Due to the strong fear of isolation, people will hunt for affection.

Carlisle's choice to create companions for himself has been a controversial philosophical issue surrounding the Twilight books. Was it right for him to change people into vampires, or not? Psychologically, however, Carlisle's choice is not a selfish or moral matter. His survival depended on it. You see, Carlisle's actions allude to some of the most famous research in psychology about the nature of love. Scientific evidence proves that people and animals cannot live without affection. Dr Harry Harlow, a psychology professor and American Psychological Association gold-medal winner, was the first scientist to prove that not only is a lack of love devastating – it is fatal.

Traditional behavior scientists have always assumed that people's primary drives are physical ones – hunger, thirst, elimination, pain, and sex. Emotional drives, like love and affection, were considered secondary and far less important. Earlier behavior scientists would argue that Carlisle did not need to create companions to ensure his survival. Before the 1950s, very little was known about the nature of love and the effects of emotional contact on health and life expectancy. It was psychology research that provided evidence that many creatures, especially highly evolved organisms, cannot live without love. Affectionate bonding is essential for the development of healthy adult behavior.

Just as Carlisle created companions for himself such as Edward and Esme, Dr Harlow's research on primates found that intimate emotional contact with others – love – was critical to existence. It has long been observed that human babies cling to their carers and become attached to cuddly things. Dr Harlow observed that young rhesus monkeys raised in laboratories with no mothers became very attached to pieces of cloth in their cages. The most shocking observation of all was that baby monkeys raised in wire cages without soft cloths died within five days of birth. This provided scientific evidence that affectionate attachment is essential for survival. When young monkeys were given a choice of a care figure (a 'wire figure' that provided milk mechanically or a 'cloth figure' that did not provide food), the babies always clung to the soft cloth figures, even though the wire figures fed them. Just as human babies cling to parents when they feel frightened, Harlow found that young monkeys sought affectionate contact from cuddly cloth figures when frightened. Harlow's extraordinary experiments provided hard-hitting proof that the deprivation of affection is deadly. A lack of love kills.

Carlisle's choice to bond affectionately with others also fits well with existential psychology. Martin Heidegger, for example, argues that 'one's existence is a network of meaningful involvements' and that this 'care structure' is 'the very core of what it means to be a human-being: that people care, that the people, places, and things with which one is involved inevitably matter'. In other words, people's relationships with the outside world influence life quality. Caring relationships are so important that they alter a person's psychological experience of time and space.

When Bella interacts affectionately with Edward, she feels lost in time, as if in a trance: 'When I was with him, the time and the place were such a muddled blur that I completely lost track of both' (*Twilight*, p190). The psychologist Mihaly Csikszentmihalyi calls this positive and absorbing experience 'flow'.

The experience of space can also change, zooming in and out depending on how 'familiar' people are with their surroundings. For example, the first time Bella ever saw the Cullen house it looked 'three stories tall . . . very open, and very large' (*Twilight*, p281). Once Bella got used to the house it became a snugger, cozier place. Resting on a couch in the lounge room next to Edward, his family and Jacob, Bella felt '*complete* . . . like all my family is together' (*Breaking Dawn*, p273). Without a doubt, the field of psychology provides powerful insight into Dr Cullen's savvy survival strategies and his relentless hunt for affection.

## A Vampire Foster Family: The Cullens

### Let's Stick Together

Let's meet our favorite vampire family – psychologically. We already know that each member of the Cullen clan has a unique personality. There's the compassionate Carlisle, his caring wife Esme, introspective Edward, Alice the extraverted live-wire, the fragile Jasper, and a resolute Rosalie married to easy-going Emmett. What's more, each family member has a unique supernatural 'gift'. For example, Edward reads minds while Alice can see the future. Despite such salient individual differences, however, the Cullens' most striking psychological dynamic is their powerful drive to stick together as a family. The Cullens are a cohesive group and a model foster family who show that love is a lot stronger than blood lust. The first time Bella visits the Cullen family residence, Edward's parents make her feel right at home and she is thrilled when Alice kisses her on the cheek to welcome her (*Twilight*, p283). A sense that you belong to a cohesive group is a reassuring feeling and a significant source of happiness. Many animal species affiliate, collecting in groups, flocks or schools to migrate or search for food.

## Group Roles

Not only does each Cullen have a distinctive personality and a unique gift, each family member has a valuable group role that preserves the family and keeps it together. Of course, Dr Cullen appears to play a formal role leading the family. He is the oldest and most experienced vampire and he has created four family members (Edward, Esme, Rosalie, and Emmett). However, *informal* roles also strongly influence how a group behaves and what it achieves. Each individual member has a different interaction style and way of doing things. In fact, social experts have identified three types of informal roles that influence small groups such as the Cullen family:

- Task roles – these roles influence a group's completion of a goal
- Maintenance roles – these roles influence group relationships and interaction
- Disruptive roles – these roles interfere with the needs and ability of a group to reach its goals

(Source: Benne and Sheats, 1948; Mudrack and Farrell, 1995)

With regards to *task roles*, for example, individuals are naturally geared to play particular roles in a group. This includes 'energizer', 'elaborator', 'evaluator', 'coordinator', 'information-seeker', 'giver' or maybe some other role. The first time Bella visits the Cullens at their home, that meeting immediately reveals certain group dynamics and specific group roles within the Cullen family.

## Esme the Energizer

In the Cullen family, Esme seems to be the group's *energizer*. This is someone who 'stimulates group members to take action'. It was Esme who asked Edward to play the piano for Bella: 'Edward didn't tell you he was musical? . . . Well, play for her' (*Twilight*, p284). Esme also referees the family baseball game to 'keep them honest' (*Twilight*, p321) and encourages Edward to date Bella because she is 'what he wants' (*Twilight*, 322).

## Rosalie the Evaluator

Rosalie plays a very different role in the family with regard to group tasks. She appears to be the Cullen clan's *evaluator*. This is someone who 'keeps the group on track and maintains high standards'. Rosalie reveals her group role when she makes efforts to protect the family's secret – that they are vampires. As Edward explains to Bella, Rosalie 'struggles with what we are. It's hard for her to have someone on the outside know the truth' (*Twilight*, p285). As the group's guardian of high standards, Rosalie does not want the Volturi vampires to hurt her family. At the same time, Rosalie is also maintaining high standards to protect Bella's rights and freedom as a human. As Rosalie explains to Bella later: 'Can't you see that I'd trade everything I have to be you? You have the choice' (*Eclipse*, p148). Rosalie again rises as the group's 'evaluator' (the guardian of high standards) when she agrees to protect Bella's unborn child. Bella begged Rosalie to help her and then 'ran right into Rosalie's arms' at the airport (*Breaking Dawn*, p125, p163). Rosalie's 'gift' of super-tenacity enables her to be a strong and effective 'evaluator', no doubt.

## Bella the Giver

When Bella finally joins the Cullens as a vampire, she acquires her own group role within the family. Gifted with her protective supernatural 'shield' and an innate desire to care for everyone, Bella is the group's *giver* – the one who 'provides valuable information or support to a group to help the group achieve its goals'. Just like a 'butterfly', Bella emerges from her human cocoon – a dazzling otherworldly savior. Hmmm, it may interest you to know that according to ancient Slavic myth, vampires *can* change themselves into butterflies. This makes Bella a powerful icon in light of group theory.

### A Family of Wolves: Jacob's Pack

What does it feel like to be a werewolf in Twilight territory and run with a pack of wolves? To Jacob, the most important feeling of all is to be part of an affectionate family. As Jacob explains: 'There are definitely good sides to this – the speed, the freedom, the strength . . . the sense of – of *family*' (*Eclipse*, p102). Since wolves form a close-knit social structure, Native American people value 'community', and the Quileute werewolves share telepathic powers, these group-geared factors would bolster the family feeling even more.

### Autocratic Alpha?

In Twilight's family of wolves, Sam Uley leads the pack. *Eclipse* introduces him as 'the Alpha. When he tells us to do something, or not to do something . . . we can't just ignore him' (p319). If the wolves are working together as a group – hunting, protecting, whatever – it helps enormously to have a team leader to communicate information, make decisions, lead projects, coordinate activities, and resolve conflicts. This helps to minimize problems that might otherwise threaten their safety. Strong leadership is a top social rule for survival and success. In this important scene, for example, Sam shows how staunchly he leads his team:

> *Jacob,* Sam ordered . . . *You are going to fight . . . You are obligated to protect the tribe . . . You* will *perform this obligation.*
>
> My shoulders hunched as the edict crushed me . . . No member of the pack could refuse the Alpha.
>
> (*Breaking Dawn*, p188–189)

So just how well is the social order working among wolves in the Twilight Saga? Actually, not so great, it seems. The Quileute pack experiences a number of problems under Sam's leadership:

- Sam's leadership style is tough and bossy
- Sam uses intimidation and punishment to motivate team members
- Sam's stubborn attitude causes fights and quarrels among wolves
- Sam is far less tolerant of the peaceful Cullen vampires than the younger wolves

From a psychological point of view, Sam exhibits one of the least effective leadership styles – the authoritarian approach. This tough and bossy style may look powerful on the surface, but it is coercive, undesirable, and inappropriate for most group situations.

Authoritarian leaders have rigid standards for behavior which are strictly enforced using punishment. 'They expect instant and unquestioning obedience' from people and 'exert restrictive control' over others, says the *International Encyclopedia of Psychology*. Challenges to authority are simply not tolerated. The effects on young people with authoritarian parents are mostly negative – they are unhappy, socially withdrawn, distrustful, moody, impulsive, show poor self-control, and are over-rebellious or else over-dependent on others for decision-making. Children and teens show low self-esteem and are more likely to be rejected by their peers. Not a fantastic family bonding approach at all.

Eventually, Sam's bossy management style causes a permanent family breakdown. When Sam insists on killing innocent people, Jacob makes a choice to leave the pack: '*I won't follow you, Sam. Not for something wrong*' (*Breaking Dawn*, p193). After that, Seth leaves Sam's gang to follow Jacob too (*Breaking Dawn*, p196). And then Leah joins their 'crappy little renegade pack' (*Breaking Dawn*, p208). Fortunately, the field of psychology has developed and tested theories to find the best ways to manage and motivate small groups of people. Most of this research has studied how teams operate in the workplace.

## Team Building

The most popular and widely accepted theory of motivation in the workplace is expectancy theory. According to Victor Vroom, people's motivation to perform certain behaviors depends on their expectations about three things:

- Ability: 'Will I be able to do this?'
- Outcomes: 'What will I get out of doing this?'
- Attitudes: 'Will I value my behavior's outcome?'

If an Alpha wanted to lead a pack of werewolves effectively and get the most out of each group member, that leader would be wise to use a well-known technique of expectancy theory. It's called *job enrichment* and Frederick Herzberg introduced it. He argued that people have 'an innate need to grow psychologically and develop their skills' and that people enjoy work that offers 'opportunities to learn, to be responsible, and to experience a sense of achievement'. Herzberg really improved and revolutionized workplaces for mechanics, administrative staff, cleaners, assembly-line workers, managers and many other workplaces. By giving workers more challenging and interesting work, more freedom and control over the quality of results, and opportunities to participate, help make decisions, and self-schedule their own work times, people everywhere produced *more* results, achieved *better* results and felt much more *satisfied* in the workplace. Unlike Sam, the Twilight series suggests that Jacob is a democratic leader who supports the job enrichment approach. For example, when Seth joins Jacob's pack in *Breaking Dawn*:

- Jacob does not 'order' Seth around (p197)
- When Seth calls Jacob 'sir', Jacob discourages it (p197)
- Jacob states that Seth can do as he pleases (p198)
- Jacob accepts ideas from Seth which prove very helpful: 'Seth thought with me, filling in the gaps, showing the scene from another angle' (p199)
- Jacob welcomes Seth's initiatives, such as offering to '*take a look*' around for danger (p200)

This democratic and enriching leadership style shows that Jacob values self-expression, that he acknowledges individual rights and strengths, and that he encourages others to think for themselves. No wonder werewolves like Seth and Leah join Jacob and stick with him.

## The Eagle's Test

A Native American tale about eagles has survived centuries to bring you a very special psychological message about love. In fact, this Wintu tribal story is helping young people today to beat depression and suicide. Although relationships are crucial to health and happiness, many people are not sure how to identify positive personality characteristics in others or assess a person's relationship potential. A teenage girl became depressed and suicidal after her boyfriend cheated on her and then dumped her. This 16-year-old needed some clear strategies in mind to determine if a guy would make a good boyfriend or not. The eagle tale helped to introduce the advantages of developing smart partner-picking skills. This is the tale of 'How the Eagle Chooses Her Mate':

When a female eagle is ready to choose a mate, many keen suitors appear. To pick the best possible companion, she studies the male eagles carefully and then follows this special sequence of steps:

- She selects one to fly with.
- If she likes the way he flies, she will find a small stick, grab it, and fly high in the sky with it.
- She then drops the stick to see if the male can catch it.
- If the male eagle catches the stick, she finds a bigger stick, flies higher with it, and then drops it again.
- Each time the male catches a stick, she gets a bigger one, flies higher yet, and drops it for him to catch.
- The last stick is the biggest and heaviest one of all, which she drops from the highest point in the sky.
- If the male fails to catch a stick, she flies away from him to signal that the test is over – he has failed.
- The female eagle 'tests' new eagles this way again, until she finds an eagle who can catch all the sticks.
- She chooses this eagle to be her lifelong mate.

(Source of story: Bates, 2006. In Garnier and Yapko, 2010)

'So how can a big bird of prey improve *my* love life?' you ask.

Well, as the wise Wintu elders explain, one day the female eagle and her mate will have eaglets, high on a cliff somewhere. If an eaglet falls from its nest, the survival of the species depends on the male's ability to catch the falling babies. The female eagle's long and tough partner-picking process highlights the benefits of getting to know people, and their strengths and weaknesses, properly. If you use the same smart strategies, you will reduce your chances of choosing a partner who cannot or will not look after you. If you develop effective relationship skills, you will increase your chances of making love last. If you want to hunt down true love, you will find it if you look with sharp eagle-eyes for that special someone. At any rate, this story helped to decrease the teenage girl's feelings of depression and suicide considerably. It showed her that if you want to increase your success in relationships, it helps to assess a person's boyfriend/girlfriend potential carefully and systematically. This can help you to make a much more informed and purposeful decision about people, rather than getting hooked up with someone without really knowing why.

Did you know that in England, Prince William and Kate Middleton dated each other for *eight years* before getting married on April 29, 2011? Both William and Kate were patient and careful about choosing each other. They took time to self-disclose, got to know each other well in different situations, and developed a passionate, intimate *and* committed love. As such, this charming prince and his royal bride have maximized their chances of long-term love and living happily ever after. That's a lot of stick-snatching work for the Duke of Cambridge. *Phew!*

4

# I Bite: Twilight's Risk-Taking Behavior

*Yes, risk-taking is inherently failure prone.*
*Otherwise, it would be called sure-thing-taking.*
- Tim McMahon, punk rock vocalist

## Why Take Risks?

What do these Twilight adventures have in common?

- Riding a motorbike too fast – first lesson, no helmet
- Jumping off a cliff into the sea – during a wild storm
- Kissing a human neck when you're a vampire
- Punching a werewolf in the face

Answer: A desire for thrills, spills and danger. Adrenaline and neurotransmitters partying in the body and brain. All these situations involve *risk-taking behavior*. In Bella's infamous words: 'I was going to be as reckless as I could possibly manage' (*New Moon*, p147).

Absolutely everyone takes risks. A sneak peek, a bold stare, a do or dare. A leap before looking or a move without thinking. A go at it, a run for it, or a crazy crack to *be* it. A risk is a taste of forbidden adventure; it's like taking a big 'bite' out of life. To take a risk means to do something when the results are not certain or the outcomes are not necessarily positive. Some risks are dangerous and deadly, as many adventures from the Twilight Saga show.

These days, risk-taking is a hot topic. This makes Twilight's take on risk-taking all the more timely, instructive and real.

Already, some characters in the Twilight books have made risqué moves that have been discussed and debated on the internet. So, why not analyze the exploits of Bella, Edward, Jacob and friends in a way that informs and empowers you psychologically?

Consider this controversial thrill-seeking adventure, for example:

> The gear caught and wrenched me forward.
>
> And I was flying . . .
>
> The adrenaline coursed through my body, tingling in my veins.
>
> (*New Moon*, p186)

Bella gets an 'adrenaline rush' on her first motorbike lesson. Are her actions and sensations good? Healthy? Evil? Brainless? Crazy? Actually, Bella illustrates normal teenage behavior. Of course, not wearing a helmet and revving the '@#&$!' out of the throttle is a worry!

## It's Normal Behavior

Some critics have slammed the Twilight books for promoting inappropriate risk-taking. But an important side to taking risks is that it is normal human behavior. According to drive theory in psychology, all living organisms, including people – like Bella – have a natural need to seek stimulation from the environment to keep the body balanced and healthy. Without drives, there would be no learning or behavioral progress because satisfying drives is what reinforces learning and enables adaptation. Without drives – a desire to do things and tackle challenges – there could be no behavioral response, for a drive activates behavioral potentials into performance (*The International Encyclopedia of Psychology*). Dr Joseph Rey is a Director of Child and Adolescent Mental Health Services and a Clinical Professor of Child and Adolescent Psychiatry at the University of Sydney. This is what he says about teenage risk-taking: 'Testing limits – family's, society's and their own – is an important experience through which they learn the boundaries of their skills and consolidate their self-esteem.' In other words, if people never got any thrills or spills or made stupid mistakes to learn from, their lives would be severely diminished. Life would feel as if Alec was forcing his evil vampire 'gift' on you – a creeping mist that 'makes you feel nothing. Absolutely nothing . . . he cuts off your senses . . . Total sensory deprivation' (*Breaking Dawn*, p533). Without risks, life would be nothing at all.

Risk-taking teaches people how to express behavior, develop skills, deal with challenges, and manage situations by themselves, which is essential for survival, autonomy and normal human development.

A few examples of healthy and socially acceptable risk-taking from the Twilight Saga:

- Bella moves from Arizona to live with her father in Forks.
- Bella and Edward fall in love with each other.
- Edward takes Bella home to meet his vampire family. *Big* risk! (Will they like her?)
- Jacob tells Bella he loves her.
- Charlie Swan the Police Chief fights crime every day.
- Due to sleet and snow in Forks, residents drive cars on icy slippery roads. Ooooh . . . a bit risky.

As you can see, some risks are a normal and necessary part of life. In fact, as these timeless quotes suggest, it can be a lot more risky *not* to take risks:

- 'To win you have to risk loss' (Jean-Claude Killy)
- 'A ship in a harbor is safe – but that is not what ships are for' (John A Shedd, *Salt from My Attic*)
- 'You'll always miss 100% of the shots you don't take'

(Wayne Gretzky)

- 'This nation was built by men who took risks – pioneers who were not afraid of the wilderness, business men who were not afraid of failure, scientists who were not afraid of the truth, thinkers who were not afraid of progress, dreamers who were not afraid of action' (Brooks Atkinson)
- 'Behold the turtle. He makes progress only when he sticks his neck out' (James Bryant Conant)

If you don't take risks, you don't experience, you don't learn, you don't grow, and you don't live.

## Positive Risk-Taking

A few thrill-seeking stunts in the Twilight books have been called pretty 'brainless'. But don't let the critics eclipse the best. The Twilight Saga is *essentially* a tale about taking important and meaningful risks in the name of love, happiness, and making a positive difference in the world. A main theme in the Twilight series is that the only way to achieve great results is to take great risks and make great sacrifices. Important examples of brave and responsible risk-taking from the Twilight series are these:

- Edward saves Bella from being squashed by a car at school.
- Dr Cullen takes a risk saving the lives of Edward, Esme, and other dying humans by turning them into vampires.
- Edward risks offending the ruling Volturi vampires by dating a human.
- Bella is willing to die as a human in order to become a vampire. A life without Edward and his love is the worst possible option to her.
- Fighting for love, life, freedom and what you believe in is always risky and dangerous, whether it's against newborn vampires, Volturi dictators, or human aggressors in real life.

People who do not take any risks disempower themselves. They shrink their potential to achieve autonomy, leadership, and success in life. They forego opportunities to learn, change and flourish. *Risk Takers* is a Canadian television documentary series, which profiles people in dangerous professions. The show originally aired on Discovery Channel Canada, and also airs on the North American channel Discovery HD Theater. Young people, in particular, benefit from learning to take risks because they learn how to manage situations. Taking chances elevates people to greater psychological maturity. The happiest and healthiest people are risk-takers. Positive risk-taking is a must-have ingredient for a rich and rewarding life.

## A Heroic Quality

What will you risk to experience victory?

How far would you go to achieve something incredible?

Would you put yourself in harm's way to protect someone you love?

Are there some things you would sacrifice in order to get what you really, really, really want?

Not all risky behavior is mad, bad or thoughtless. In fact, some psychologists have found that risk-taking is an important quality of *heroism*. Many heroes – leaders, humanitarians, police officers, soldiers, international charity workers, and Twilight characters like Bella, Edward and Jacob – have put themselves in stressful or perilous situations to protect what is truly important. A number of psychologists who reviewed personal qualities that characterize 'heroism' identified these six heroic traits: 'courage', 'strength', 'honesty', 'kindness', 'generosity', and 'risk-taking'. One researcher who studies Type-T personalities (those exhibiting perpetual thrill-seeking behavior) reported that heroes are most willing to take risks and place themselves in danger to achieve meaningful outcomes (*Psychology Today*, 2010). The risk-taking trait of heroes is what helps them to function under extreme pressure or adversity. A hero protects what is good and right and would risk his or her life to save a loved one.

Compared to unconstructive risk-takers, genuine heroes are positive psychology people. They take risks and fight fiercely for what they believe in, but their behavior is geared towards goodness and positive values. For example, they fight for justice and freedom, not greed or persecution. Martin Luther King Jr and Mother Teresa are true-life heroes who worked tirelessly and risked their lives to support worthwhile social causes. And in the Twilight Saga? Bella sacrifices her life time and time again to keep Edward, her parents and the Cullen family safe. Edward and Jacob also risk their lives to protect Bella, their families and their lifestyles. A true hero will take big risks to support big causes.

## Too Risky?

## Twilight's Risky Business

Of course, the Twilight books describe negative risk-taking too. For example:

- Bella tests the town – she approaches a group of intoxicated and intimidating men at Port Angeles (*Twilight*, p110).
- Edward entombs himself in a psychological crypt – he puts his life at great risk when he travels to another country, isolating his suicidal self from people who care about him and who can keep him safe (*New Moon*, p419).
- Jacob shows his claws – his temper flares up easily and regularly once he turns into an angry teen wolf (*New Moon*, p311–312, p345; *Breaking Dawn*, p61, p150). As Jacob tells Bella: 'It's not safe for *you*. If I get too mad . . . too upset . . . you might get hurt' (*New Moon*, p311).

Nevertheless, these negative risk-taking behaviors don't

automatically make our favorite Twilight characters bad or weak characters. If you look *underneath* the surface, Bella, Edward and Jacob offer important psychological insights into issues that drive young people to take negative risks. For example, a stressful past, a difficult home life, or feelings of insecurity can lead to dangerous risk-taking behavior among teenagers in real life. Family conflict and stress at school can increase self-destructive behaviors such as problematic drug and alcohol use. Instead of criticizing people who take risks, a much more powerful strategy is to understand why they are doing it.

In Bella's case, she experienced past stress when her parents separated. This may have affected her ability to be self-confident, trust others or attach to others. At school, boys like Mike and Eric keep pressuring her for dates and attention, which she clearly dislikes. Other students at school, like Jessica, act more like bullies than friends at times.

As a result of various social and environmental influences, a young person like Bella may adopt a riskier lifestyle to escape pain, pressure or loneliness. Edwards supports this theory when he tells Bella: 'You are a magnet for trouble' (*Twilight*, p151). There are countless ways to take harmful risks. Some people might use alcohol or drugs heavily to de-stress. Other people deliberately harm themselves to ease emotional hurt (e.g. self-cutting). Friends affect teen risk-taking behavior enormously. For example, Bella jumped off a cliff into the sea only after watching a group of young guys from La Push do it. This is a good example of copycat risk-taking behavior, which occurs often in real life and involves behaviors as lethal as suicide. As you can see, a range of social influences encourage young people to take negative risks. This doesn't make negative risk-takers bad people. Rather, it suggests that good people may be suffering badly. By getting some support that addresses the underlying problems, people can effectively reduce harmful risk-taking behaviors.

## Bella's Big Dive

Bella's risk-taking behavior takes a dark and deadly turn in *New Moon*. When Bella feels she can't cope anymore without Edward, when her feelings of emptiness and depression overwhelm her, and her relationship breakup with Edward 'gets' to her, her pain pushes her to the psychological edge:

> I knew that this was the stupidest, most reckless thing I had done yet . . .
>
> I stepped out to the edge . . .
>
> And I flung myself off the cliff.
>
> (*New Moon*, p359)

Bella didn't dive off a cliff for 'fun', to make an exciting 'Coca Cola' TV commercial, or as a military training exercise with a pack of Quileute wolves. She took the big plunge because she was feeling depressed and desperate. She wanted to hear the sound of Edward's voice in her mind. Alone at the top of the cliffs with a mind muddled with depressing thoughts, her idea to escape pain became more dangerous than ever. A strong current dragged Bella beneath the freezing water where she decided she 'didn't want to fight anymore' anyway and 'the whole dying thing was pretty bearable' (*New Moon*, p361). This information suggests that Bella was mentally fragile at the time she dived into the sea. Sinking in the cold water, sinking deeper into danger, Bella's big dive almost became a fully successful suicide.

## Thrill-Seeker Dies

Another risk-taking adventure, similar to Bella's, is not an action scene from the rugged cliffs of La Push. It is a true-life event. In 2009 a '25-year-old Columbia man died after he jumped off a 60-foot-high cliff into the Huzzah Creek in Crawford County', says the *Columbia Daily Tribune*, a Missouri newspaper. A guy named Garrick 'jumped into 6-foot deep water and hit his head. He was pronounced dead while being flown by helicopter to St. John's Hospital,' the state water patrol Sergeant Jerry Callahan confirmed. According to witnesses 'there was quite a bit of alcohol use involved,' said Callahan. This is a very sad and unfortunate event.

As the cliff-diving actions of Bella and real-life people like Garrick suggest, young people in their teens and twenties are high-risk groups for dangerous risk-taking behavior. But this doesn't make the risk-takers stupid or irresponsible, even if *they* describe themselves as 'reckless'. From a psychological viewpoint, repeated dangerous risk-taking behavior is usually fueled by emotional distress or a psychological crisis. People who are impulsive, seek danger, and harm themselves repeatedly may suffer from mental health problems. This includes strong depression or anxiety. It's a bit risky to judge the negative risk-taking behavior of Twilight characters, and real people, too hastily. This is because deeper psychological issues could be involved. If anything, people need information, support and guidance in relation to risk-taking and how to manage risks. Fortunately, a range of good risk-reducing and control-enhancing strategies abound. You can find good risk-reducing tips in recent role models like Edward, in the field of psychology, and in old eerie myths.

## Tips from a Vampire's Forest

> Soon we were hemmed in with trees, which in places arched right over the roadway till we passed as through a tunnel . . . We could hear the rising wind, for it moaned and whistled through the rocks, and the branches of the trees crashed together as we swept along.
>
> (Bram Stoker, *Dracula*)

A man called Jonathan Harker is describing his trip in a horse-drawn carriage one night through the vampire woodlands of

East Europe. He is on his way to meet the notorious vampire Count Dracula who lives in a castle in Transylvania.

Long before there was a science of psychology, people used dark myths and eerie tales for centuries to:

- Teach life skills
- Teach survival skills
- Promote safety
- Encourage positive behavior
- Discourage foolish and dangerous risk-taking
- Suggest ways to decrease and control risk

In a saga about vampires, it would be rude to ignore old Slavic myths that emerged in vampire territory. They were, after all, designed to increase people's control over danger.

## The Lisovyk's Tricks

From the banks of the dark blue Dnipro river of Ukraine to the Velebit mountains of Croatia to the icy-rocky highlands of Russia, many Slavic myths from wild areas reinforce risk-management strategies embraced by the Twilight series. If you want to experience dangerous situations – and survive – then it might be worth heeding the 'risk-taking rules' suggested in these myths. To get 'out of the woods' alive, so to speak, here's a lesson from a strange supernatural creature called the *lisovyk*. Every forest in Ukraine is run by one – a spooky sprite that can manifest as a shabby old man, a giant with horns, a tall tree, a tiny blade of grass or maybe even a fierce animal. He dwells in the most desolate places, including uninhabited caves or deserted huts in winter, singing and whistling to himself. The lisovyk controls the natural riches of the forest and all the forest animals obey him. Wolves are his most loyal helpers.

A lisovyk likes to get people lost in the forest. He can interfere with a person's sense of direction, especially if you are wandering in the forests and mountains *alone*. One lonely traveler in Ukraine reported that he ended up 'doing circles in the Carpathians. In spite of having a compass and knowing the place well I, instead of getting to my destination' was lured elsewhere. 'I could not find my tent. I kept looking for it for hours. The moment I sat down to rest, the local lisovyk would start making all kinds of frightening noises, screaming and whooping which sent shivers down my spine. It went on like this until morning,' reports Roman Malko, who lived to tell the tale.

So, what risk rules do lisovyk tricks suggest?

- Don't walk too far into the forest.
- Don't explore wild places alone.
- To make your trek a treat, hike with others to increase safety.
- Prepare thoroughly – take emergency food, safety supplies and protective equipment.
- Whenever you're in vampire country, maximize safety and minimize danger.

By the way, I am not trying to be over-theatrical here. I have been inside Ukrainian forests where vampires are said to roam. One sunny summer's day at noon, all it took was one second for the forest to shroud me in cold shadows and utter darkness. The message from the vampire's forest is a good one – it pays to control risk.

## Twilight's Best Risk-Control Secrets

You would be mad to miss Twilight's best self-control secrets modeled by a cool and classy vampire. In fact, Edward and the Twilight books are becoming really famous for using some of the best-known psychology techniques to control and manage risk. If you know some smart risk-management techniques, then just like Edward and his friends, you too can increase control in your life.

## Edward's Cool Control

'You are exactly my brand of heroin' (*Twilight*, p234–235).

Despite the fact that Edward finds Bella as tempting and irresistible as an illegal 'drug' – both sexually *and* nutritionally – he *never* gives in to his powerful urges. Edward helps to show everyone that self-regulation is a psychological strength that involves controlling impulses, feelings, thoughts, and behaviors.

Edward holds hands, touches, embraces, and kisses Bella, and spends time alone with her. Even though Edward has practiced hunting down his substance of choice (human blood) and preying on warm-blooded creatures for over one hundred years, he never 'loses control'. This is why Edward calls himself a 'sick, masochistic lion' (*Twilight*, p240) – he continually encounters a substance he really desires, yet he restrains himself from using it. As Edward warns Bella: 'I can never, never afford to lose any kind of control when I'm with you' (*Twilight*, p271). Despite the craziest vampire cravings, not only does Edward not drink Bella's blood, he chooses to abstain from sex (Edward wants to marry Bella first; it's a 19th-century thing). This is despite strong peer pressure – like sexual advances – from Bella. This 17-year-old vampire initiates, develops, and masters a superior degree of *self*-control and *other*-respect. Edward is anything but an impulsive and thoughtless predator. He is a cool control protégé.

A recent news story reported that Edward is a very positive role model of self-control for young people. This is because Edward excels at mastering urges, cravings and addictive behaviors. In the 2009 report '*Twilight* is a positive psychology film: Edward and self-control', psychologists praised Edward's behavior, describing *Twilight* as a 'very important positive psychology film'.

In one scene from the *Twilight* movie, Edward (Robert Pattinson) tries to alert Bella (Kristen Stewart) that he is dangerous, saying that: 'If you were smart, you'd stay away from me.' This kind of behavior makes Edward 'a paragon for self-regulation in the way in which he maintains exquisite, healthy control of his emotions, impulses, and instincts,' say psychologists Jeremy Clyman and Ryan Niemiec. 'Edward tries hard to display self-control as he faces a crescendo of challenges in which he must continue to develop his 'muscle' of self-control,' they say. Although Edward struggles in numerous adventures and doubts he can control himself, he succeeds every time. Edward the good vampire shows that anyone who uses the right skills can achieve superior self-control.

## Who Is Twilight's Control Star?

'Carlisle . . . was the only one who could bear the smell of my blood without suffering from the intense temptation' (*New Moon*, p34).

The Twilight Saga's self-control superstar would have to be Dr Carlisle Cullen. After all, he does have an unfair supernatural advantage: he has been a vampire for more than 300 years. After learning, practicing, and establishing the art of effective self-regulation for over three centuries, he can cruise through a blood bath at the Forks hospital's emergency department without slurping one delicious drop.

In fact, superior self-control is why so many people love the Cullen vampires. They restrain their desires to kill and feed on humans. In particular, Dr C shows superior control over destructive behavior. He has transcended his primitive vampire urges and has found a way to survive without preying on people. Most vampires provoke feelings of horror and fear because of their inability to control their bloodlust. The brutal and bloodthirsty urges are what make vampires so scary in the first place. Unlike the Cullens, most other vampires cannot or will not control their aggressive impulses to kill, devour humans, and drink their blood. The Cullens' cool control comforts and inspires us, and their compassion not to hurt humans wins our hearts.

## Dr C's Secret

One of Dr C's best self-control scenes is at Bella's 18th birthday party. Bella cuts her finger on some paper and then falls into a pile of smashed crystal at the Cullen house, cutting herself more deeply. Dr C shows no signs of distress as he attends to Bella's bleeding, removing sharp pieces of glass from her arm (*New Moon*, p33). Although Dr C is a vampire, he is cool, calm and collected as he treats the bloody wound (*New Moon*, p34). With perfectly steady hands, he stitches up deep cuts in Bella's arm and has a calm conversation with her. In particular, Dr C deals with the smell of Bella's blood without the slightest signs of losing control. What's his secret? 'Years and years of practice . . . I barely notice the scent anymore' (*New Moon*, p34), he explains to Bella. To stay in control, the best tip of all is to *practice, practice, practice* positive skills as much as possible. This makes sound Dr C sense.

## Twilight Teaches Relapse Prevention

So what are Twilight's best self-control techniques? How does Edward use his mind to master matter? When it comes to control, can human folk get as good as the Cullens? An analysis of Twilight adventures from a psychological angle happens to reveal some of the most powerful and effective self-regulation techniques from the field of relapse prevention.

## What Is Relapse Prevention?

Relapse Prevention is a psychological approach that aims to 'increase the awareness and choice of a person in relation to his/her drug use, developing coping skills and self-control' and 'fostering a greater sense of confidence and self-efficacy' (Turning Point Alcohol and Drug Centre, 2000). In other words, relapse prevention tries to stop people from letting addictive substances and harmful urges control their lives. Relapse prevention also shows people how to increase their control over risky and harmful situations. The Twilight Saga is so good at mentioning effective relapse prevention techniques to control bloodlust that you are hardly aware you are learning them.

A popular and powerful relapse prevention approach is the Marlatt Model. This model is used to help people master problems like addiction, aggression, and other self-destructive behaviors. The Twilight books show Edward and other characters applying a number of Marlatt Model techniques, which help people to:

- Deal with high-risk situations with skill
- Control cravings and addictive behaviors
- Improve self-efficacy (self-confidence)
- Make lifestyle changes that reduce the need for substances
- Undertake healthy activities
- Manage slips or 'lapses' to prevent long-term 'relapses'
- Minimize harm
- Learn positive social skills

(Source: Daley and Marlatt, 1997)

Not only does Edward illustrate strategies from the Marlatt model, this approach can help good vampires like Jasper to control his urges and not 'relapse' again the way he did at Bella's birthday party.

### The 5 Ws: A Functional Analysis

To reach the highest Twilight relapse-prevention standard, one of the first helpful things to know is that people who are addicted to drugs, alcohol, food, 'human blood' or other substances do not use those substances at random. Substance use is a pattern of behavior, triggered by certain factors. If a person identifies the things that 'trigger' the urges and cravings, that person can put in strategies to manage those triggers. For example, Edward's urge to drink Bella's blood is much stronger when he is with her in a 'warm room' because this makes the scent stronger (*Twilight*, p236).

Discovering which factors put someone at risk of using a substance and describing a person's pattern of behavior is called a *functional analysis* of behavior. You are discovering how a person's unique habits actually work or *function*. Anyone can find out how their urges function, simply by using these 5 Ws:

- WHEN is the substance used? (what times, how long, how much is used)
- WHERE is the substance used? (the places and situations)
- WHY is the substance used? (personal reasons, certain external cues and internal emotional states can trigger cravings)
- WHO is around when the substance is used? WHO provides the substance? (e.g. drug dealer)
- WHAT happens after the substance is used? (the effects of using)

When people use the 5 Ws to monitor the way they use substances, this helps them to identify meaningful behavior patterns. If a vegetarian vampire says: 'I get strong urges to drink human blood', that's not particularly informative. But if a vampire works out that: 'I get urges to drink human blood at night, when I'm alone, especially after quarreling with a werewolf', this description of substance use is much more useful because it identifies the reasons and circumstances behind the substance use.

In the Twilight series, Edward identifies some high-risk situations for himself. For example, Edward explains to Bella: 'Sometimes we make mistakes. Me, for example, allowing myself to be alone with you' (*Twilight*, p163). Later on, Edward says: 'It's wrong. It's not safe. I'm dangerous, Bella' (*Twilight*, p166). Edward is trying to let Bella know that his desire to drink her blood (his favorite brand of heroin) is strongest when he is *alone* with her.

Another high-risk situation Edward identifies is being exposed to blood. As Alice explains to Bella:

> We're also like sharks in a way. Once we taste the blood, or even smell it for that matter, it becomes very hard to keep from feeding. Sometimes impossible. So you see, to actually bite someone, to taste the blood, it would begin the frenzy.
> (*Twilight*, p362)

The sight, smell, or taste of blood makes it much harder for vampires to control their blood-drinking urges. The message? It's much harder to stop drinking blood, or whatever drug it is you crave, after you've had an initial 'taste'.

To show you how the 5 Ws can be used to map behavior and help people to increase control, here is a table functionally analyzing the time Jasper lost control at Bella's birthday party:

| Antecedent Situation | Thoughts | Feelings Sensations | Behaviour | Consequences |
|---|---|---|---|---|
| **Where was I?<br>Who was with me?<br>What was happening?**<br><br>***Jasper*** *– was at home with family, celebrating Bella's birthday* | **What was I thinking?**<br><br>*A thought that may have flashed through Jasper's mind: "I must drink Bella's blood NOW! It smells bloody good!"* | **How was I feeling?<br>What signals did I get from my body?**<br><br>*Jasper may have felt overwhelmed, tense, staring at the blood.* | **What did I do?<br>What did I use?<br>How much did I use?<br>What devices did I use?<br>What did other people around me do?**<br><br>Jasper's behaviours:<br>*– Lunged at Bella*<br>*– Fought with his brothers*<br>*– Smashed up dishes and furniture*<br>*– His family had to restrain him* | **What happened after?<br>How did I feel right after?<br>How did other people react to my actions?<br>Any other consequences?**<br><br>Jasper:<br>*– Felt "upset with himself" (NM, p32) and "very unhappy" (NM, p43)*<br>*– Made others sad*<br>*– Embarrassed, guilty*<br>*– Ruined the party ☹* |

As Jasper helps to show, a functional analysis of behavior helps to capture patterns and identify areas where knowledge and skills are most needed. In Jasper's case, he definitely needs others to support him. Jasper is not yet strong enough or experienced enough to control his urges by himself.

## Edward's Top 10 Lust-Busters

### Build Killer Skills

Throughout the Twilight Saga, Edward intensely craves Bella's blood, but holds himself back. He learns to control his burning thirst. According to the Marlatt Model, some of the most effective strategies to control cravings in unavoidable high-risk situations are the ones that Edward likes to use such as:

- Avoiding or leaving the situation
- Repeating motivational statements aloud
- Expressing thoughts and feelings
- Contacting support people
- Rehearsing helpful behavior

Despite his heightened sensory perception as a vampire, Edward shows exactly how to put Marlatt Model lust-busters into action. In an early scene from the *Twilight* book, when Edward finds himself sitting next to Bella in biology class, he sits as far as possible from Bella, he doesn't talk to her, he tries not to look at her, and he leaves class quickly when it finishes (*Twilight*, p20–24). Bella assumes that Edward hates her and finds her revolting. What psychology's favorite vampire is really showing, however, is admirable self-control over his dangerous and destructive impulses.

As Edward shows, people can increase their control over harmful impulses, a substance's influence, and cope effectively with high-risk situations. How? The best way to is to build killer skills, practicing and using techniques recommended by experts such as those at the Turning Point Alcohol and Drug Centre (2000). To increase your self-control skills, here are ten top lust-busters Edward uses in the Twilight Saga.

## 1. Delay Skills

When Edward kisses Bella for the first time, he uses a decision delay technique: 'Edward hesitated to test himself, to see if this was safe, to make sure he was still in control of his need' (*Twilight*, p247). Other examples of Edward using delay skills:

- 'Give me a moment,' he called . . . After ten incredibly long seconds, he walked back' (*Twilight*, p231).
- 'Wait a moment, please' (*Twilight*, p247).
- 'Be patient, Bella' (*Eclipse*, p395).

Everyone who gets cravings struggles between the temptation to engage in risky behavior (e.g. to use substances, be aggressive, act on impulse) and the choice not to. Sometimes, the more you try to battle it out, the more anxious and weary you become and the more severe your craving gets. But if you *delay* the decision and put it off – for a brief moment, a minute, an hour or longer – this will help you to control your urge.

To cope with strong urges, this decision delay skill is also called 'urge surfing'. People can gain control over strong urges by 'surfing' their urges. As Turning Point Alcohol and Drug Centre explains:

> Using the imagery of ocean waves, people are encouraged to let cravings occur, peak and pass. The purpose is not to make the cravings disappear, but to experience them in a different way that evokes less anxiety and is thus easier to ride out . . . As cravings and urges are like waves – building to a peak and then declining – delaying a decision to use may allow the craving to pass, and decrease the chance of a lapse.

It's a bit like pressing PAUSE just when you think you're about to binge drink, use drugs, bite someone's neck, hit someone, or jump off a cliff.

The decision-delay technique, or urge surfing, works with a number of behaviors. For example, psychiatrist Dr Judith Orloff offers these strategies to diffuse and delay *anger* and *aggression*:

- When you're upset, pause, and slowly count to ten – to offset the adrenaline surge of anger. Wait before you speak. Take a few deep breaths. Count to ten (or to fifty if necessary) slowly and silently. Seize the moment to reorder your thoughts before doing something you may seriously regret.
- Take time to cool off. To calm down your neurotransmitters further, take some time out, a few hours if needed. If you're feeling furious, go to a peaceful place to lower your stress level. Reduce external stimulation. Dim the lights. Listen to beautiful music. Meditate. Do yoga or exercise to remove anger from your system.

By delaying an urge, you don't have to fight the urge. This boosts your self-control more easily.

### 2. Refusal Skills

Practicing and polishing up one's refusal skills – the art of saying 'no' to drugs and risky behaviors – helps enormously to boost personal control. In the Twilight Saga, Edward excels at refusal and saying 'no' assertively in verbal *and* nonverbal ways. This includes dodging unwanted sexual advances from Bella:

- When Edward starts feeling uncomfortable kissing Bella: 'He staggered back, breaking my grip effortlessly' (*Twilight*, p317).
- When Edward's sexual desire and the urge to drink human

blood get too strong: 'He pushed me away with gentle, firm hands' (*New Moon*, p51).

- When things get too heated sexually and the temptation to bite Bella gets too strong, Edward abstains: 'He started to push me away' (*Eclipse*, p167).
- Edward evades Bella's sexual invitation by holding Bella a bit 'tighter, restraining. He sighed. "Must I always be the responsible one?"'(*Eclipse*, p171).
- When Bella gets too sexually aroused, Edward refuses to give in to a desire that could kill her: 'He pushed me away at once' (*Eclipse*, p393).
- In this bedroom scene, Edward laments: 'Bella . . . would you *please* stop trying to take your clothes off?' and then adds '*Not tonight*' (*Eclipse*, p399).

In real life, people who want to increase control over their cravings can copy Edward's strategies to tackle drug offers, and deal with other risky situations that could cause harm. Practice refusal skills (in a safe place at first) by saying things like:

- 'I'd really appreciate your support tonight, not to offer me drugs'
- 'Could you two look out for me tonight?'
- 'I feel good at the moment, no thanks!'

A reason why so many people love Edward's character is because of his old-fashioned courtesy, respect for others, and cool self-control. Edward resists drinking human blood and having sex with Bella despite being hassled by peers, culture, and his own inner urges. Edward does not take sexual advantage of Bella nor taste his favorite brand of heroin just because he can or has the opportunity. This is a real 'twist' on modern culture that 'pressures' young people to indulge in various behaviors they don't feel ready for. Psychologically speaking, people have fallen in love with Edward's cool self-control. He tries to do what makes him feel comfortable and has other people's best interests at heart, even if he must say 'no' at times.

### 3. Positive Distraction

Cravings can occupy your mind a lot. As such, a good way to avoid this situation and control urges better is to use positive distraction techniques. This means putting your energy into other positive activities. For example:

- listen to music
- watch a favorite movie
- ring up a friend
- visit a park or the beach
- swim at the pool, go bike-riding
- take a walk with friends
- read a good book
- work out at the gym
- browse the shops

When Edward feels a strong urge to kill a group of men who were planning to attack Bella, he quickly asks Bella to: 'Distract me, please' (*Twilight*, p141). Bella then talks about a boy she is thinking of running over at school. Simple – but effective. Afterwards, Edward explains that 'It was very . . . hard – you can't imagine how hard – for me to simply take you away, and leave them . . . alive' (*Twilight*, p153). A small distraction can go a long way in helping to control a destructive urge.

A good idea is to make a list of enjoyable activities to do every day, to distract yourself in an engaging and entertaining way. An example of a positive daily timetable that could help Edward bust his bloodlust is:

1 Drive to Port Angeles, listen to new music

2 Go for a walk along the pier, take in the atmosphere – sea views, salt air, cool breeze
3 Visit a museum with my dad

If *you* want to increase control over strong urges, list three positive things that you would enjoy doing to distract yourself:

1............................
2............................
3............................

### 4. Cost/Benefit Analysis

All risky behaviors have a good side and bad side to them. These are different for every individual. If you wanted to review your risky behaviors, a useful first step would be to make a list of the positives (all the things you *like* about the risky behavior) and then list the negatives (all the things you *don't like* about your risky behavior). A cost/benefit analysis helps to increase people's control because they get to see both sides of the story. It increases people's insight into consequences too – what the risky behavior actually achieves.

If Bella had the urge to go cliff-jumping every day and she wanted to control that urge, she could consider the 'pros' and 'cons' of cliff-jumping:

Positives about cliff jumping might be:

1 It's an adrenaline rush.
2 Everyone loves 'jackass' stunts.
3 It relieves boredom.

Negatives about cliff-jumping could be:

1 I could break my neck.

2 There are safer ways to get a rush (extreme sports, other exciting activities).
3 If I die, I'll lose my chance to get back with Edward.

In fact, this is one of Edward's most powerful psychological strategies. To control his dangerous urges, he keeps reminding himself of important reasons *not* to bite Bella and drink her blood:

- 'I couldn't live with myself if I ever hurt you . . . it would be unendurable' (*Twilight*, p239).
- 'You are the most important thing to me . . . ever' (*Twilight*, p240).
- 'You didn't do anything wrong, Bella. It was my fault' (*Twilight*, p240). Here, Edward takes personal responsibility, which increases his control.
- Edward 'got over' his urge when he thought Bella had died. That situation 'changed the way I look at a lot of things' (*Eclipse*, p418).

Edward excels at self-control because he has thought about what is most important to him. The thought of losing Bella is a consequence too painful for Edward to endure. This makes it much easier for him to control his urge.

### 5. Positive Self-Talk

Using positive self-talk is a really effective way to weaken urges and strengthen control. Some good examples of Edward controlling his urges in this way are:

- 'I *can* control myself' (*Twilight*, p232).
- 'Don't be afraid . . . I *swear* not to hurt you' (*Twilight*, p232).
- Edward describes himself in a positive way to Bella: 'I'm good at it . . . being with you' (*Twilight*, p271).

- 'I made up my mind that I was strong enough, that there was no possibility at all that I would [bite]' (*Twilight*, p263).

To conquer his vampire cravings, Edward even develops his own health slogan: 'Mind over matter' (*Twilight*, p263). Making up a snappy motto is a quick and easy way to remind yourself that *you* are in charge, not the urges, the substance, or whatever it is you crave.

In literature on drug addiction, some other helpful self-talk statements are:

- 'I won't die if I don't use'
- 'This urge will go away shortly'
- 'Urges are normal; I can handle it'

By talking to yourself positively, you increase your feelings of control, confidence and mastery.

### 6. Good Role Models

When Edward drives at 100 miles an hour, Bella makes sure to let him know: 'Holy crow! . . . Slow down! . . . Are you trying to kill us?' (*Twilight*, p158). In this risky scene, Bella is a positive role model. If Edward doesn't want people to discover that he is a vampire, driving a car faster than the speed of sound isn't going to help him keep his secret safe.

Harmful behaviors such as smoking, drinking, drugging and playing dangerous games almost always take place in a peer group. This is why it's so important to stick with a good group of friends who have healthy lifestyles and make you feel safe and comfortable. As Bella helps to show, good friends can be positive influences.

Getting involved in sports and group activities is one of the best ways to meet and make friends who are more likely to be happy, healthy and well-adjusted people. *Not* having opportunities to meet good friends *increases* the chances of becoming involved with 'bad' ones. In fact, research shows that not being involved in an organized leisure activity (e.g. football, dance club, writing group) clearly increases the risk of committing crimes. If cliff-jumping or motorbike-riding without a helmet seem to be getting out of hand, then it may pay to stick with good role models, which might include joining exciting clubs.

- If you have an urge to jump off cliffs by yourself, join a rock-climbing club instead.
- If you need to control a thirst for blood, hang out with Carlisle for a while.
- If you tend to be a bit 'aggro', hang out with some cool-headed and steady people for a while. What are they doing differently from people who get angry quickly? Copy their secrets.

Positive role models make self-control much easier.

### 7. Avoid/Leave High-Risk Situations

To control his blood-drinking urges, one of Edward's best and most obvious strategies is to avoid or leave situations where the urge to 'give in' is getting too hard to handle. Check out these Edward examples:

- After Bella and Edward had their first class together 'He was out the door' (*Twilight*, p21).
- Edward was absent from school for several days (*Twilight*, p26, p32).
- 'He walked close beside me to the door, still careful not to touch me' (*Twilight*, p154).
- 'I had to run out, to get away' (*Twilight*, p236), says Edward.
- 'I resisted . . . I forced myself not to wait for you, not to

follow you . . . It was easier outside . . . to think clearly, to make the right decision' (*Twilight*, p237), Edward explains.

- 'Next morning I was in Alaska' (*Twilight*, p237), says Edward.
- Bella describes a moment when: 'I leaned closer, inhaling. And he was gone . . . he was twenty feet away' (*Twilight*, p230).

Edward skipping school for a few days is a smart decision that gives him a chance to build up his strength and self-regulation skills. When Edward does return to school, he is refreshed and better able to engage in healthy interactions with others. Avoiding people, places or events that are too tempting or too risky definitely pays off. Helpful questions to ask yourself are:

- Which of my high-risk situations can I stay away from?
- How can I do this?
- What are some good (non-risky) places to go?

Safe places I could go:

1 ..............................
2 ..............................
3 ..............................

## 8. Exposure Skills

'He came to rest with the side of his face pressed tenderly against my chest. Listening to my heart . . . "It won't be so hard again" he said' (*Twilight*, p242).

This is a great example of 'exposure'. This technique involves exposing yourself to difficult situations gradually. At the same time, you try to build up skills to control your behavior in those situations. Psychologists often use exposure strategies to help people who suffer from serious anxiety disorders, but these strategies also work well with addictive behaviors. After spending some time around Bella, Edward was able to hold her hand in the car (*Twilight*, p250). That's 'handy' exposure.

Remember, Dr Cullen didn't get good at controlling his blood-lust after one session. Practice makes perfect. Training tackles temptation. If people slowly and steadily expose themselves over and over to situations they really want to master (starting with the easiest situations first), then they *can* and *do* get as good as Dr C.

### 9. Communication Skills

To control a problem behavior, it helps to talk about it. When Edward talks honestly and openly to Bella about his cravings and urges, it increases his feelings of confidence and control. Talking about your urges to friends and family can reduce feelings of anxiety and vulnerability considerably.

- 'I crave your company too much' (*Twilight*, p233).
- 'You are *exactly* my brand of heroin' (*Twilight*, p235).
- 'The fragrance coming off your skin . . . I thought it would make me deranged' (*Twilight*, p236).

A good idea is to list a few support people to contact on a business-sized card, someone you can talk to in case of an emergency.

My support people to contact:

1 ....................................
2 ....................................
3 ....................................

Staying connected with other people and communicating openly about your feelings helps to bust lust.

## 10. Make a Plan

A powerful coping skill to increase self-control is to prepare a plan, in case you end up in a high-risk situation. The plan might include a few of your favorite lust-busting ideas. In the Twilight books, Edward definitely uses this psychological strategy to increase his self-control. On one occasion, he told Bella: 'I took precautions, hunting, feeding more than usual before seeing you again' (*Twilight*, p238). Edward's plan weakened his urges to drink Bella's blood. Another time, Edward described a plan to manage a high-risk situation that involved Bella's scent. If her scent were to overwhelm him, 'If it gets to be . . . too much, I'm fairly sure I'll be able to leave' (*Twilight*, p263).

It might be nice to help someone like Jasper who hasn't perfected self-control yet but wants to. When Bella cuts her finger at her 18th birthday party at the Cullen house, Jasper cannot control his urges:

> The paper sliced my finger . . . A single drop of blood oozed from the tiny cut. It all happened very quickly then . . . Jasper struggled . . . his wild, empty eyes focused only on me.
> (*New Moon*, p29)

How could you stop Jasper from relapsing again in the future? With a bloody good relapse-prevention plan, of course! Here is some of Jasper's information merged with a real and recent relapse-prevention plan that was designed to help a young person with bipolar affective disorder overcome out-of-control alcohol and marijuana use.

## Jasper's Plan

Early warning signs:

> Worried, anxious, withdrawn, quiet, thinking about war a lot

Things other people notice:

Nervous, fidgety, staring at human necks, fiddling with objects

Triggers:

Feeling stressed, disharmony@home, excessive noise and crowds, being around negative people

**Strategies – what can I do to help myself?**

Communicate, be around positive people, talk to a doctor (Carlisle), read fantasy books, do pleasant activities e.g. beach walk, sunset drive

What other people can do:

Talk calmly to me, go for walks with me, put on relaxing music, stop me if I try to attack people

My strengths:

Loving partner to Alice, can lead people if needed, can create a positive atmosphere around me

Daily health activities:

Morning yoga, attend Forks High School on weekdays, go on social outings with Alice on weekends, go for evening walks

Support people:

- Alice – she's always there to help me
- Carlisle – father and medical doctor

- Esme – caring mother
- Edward and Emmett – brothers

***

Thanks to a bunch of vegetarian vampires and their friends, you have acquired some of the best-ever relapse-prevention insights, knowledge and skills regarding Edward's self-control secrets!

## Bella: Queen of Control

> 'Bella, how did you do it? . . . stop hunting? . . .'
> 'It might have been someone I know!'
> (*Breaking Dawn*, p387)

As soon as Bella becomes a vampire, she is able to control her urge to hunt humans immediately and with ease. How does she do it? An important reason suggested in the scene above is her signature strength – *empathy*. Her strong psychological ability to feel for others and protect them is far stronger than her urge to hurt and kill people. Bella's positive psychological quality helps her to focus clearly on things that matter most. This helps Bella overcome her urge to drink human blood. Pretty awesome for day one as a vampire, huh?

Did you know that personal control skills are highly beneficial in many ways? Some research has found that people who show self-control achieve more in life in general. In particular, teenagers who score high on self-control measures outperform their more impulsive peers in a number of ways. This includes the area of academic performance – school/course grades, test scores, admission to competitive colleges and universities, and school attendance. Perhaps it's no coincidence that Bella gets accepted to study at a university of her choice. Her self-control skills help her to get what she wants. Anyone can liberate themselves from negative feelings, transform negative behavior patterns, create a positive life, and achieve emotional freedom by developing a few control skills. The Twilight Saga is such an inspiring book series because it offers psychological tips and techniques to manage risk and increase control. When it comes to managing urges in the wild woods of life, Bella is a cool queen of control. Someone get a tiara – Bella rules!

5

# I Suffer: Dealing with Dark Psychological Forces

*Take me disappearin' through the smoke rings of my mind . . .*
*Out to the windy beach, far from the twisted reach of crazy sorrow.*
- Bob Dylan, singer/songwriter

## Dark Forces Rising

The cold, cloudy and unsettling world of Twilight introduces some dark and troubling psychological forces:

- The 'blues'
- A serious desire to die
- Lots of nervous and anxious behavior

In other words, these three mental health issues: *depression, suicide* and *anxiety*.

Not only do these themes present a chance to analyze characters like Bella and Edward more deeply. It's a chance to understand our own inner selves. Whatever you want to call the experiences of mental suffering, one thing is for sure: these dark psychological forces don't just rise in the Twilight series. They are prevalent in real life too.

According to health sources, one in five people suffer from mental illness and 18–24-year-olds have the highest rate of mental health problems of any age group. That's the age group of the students at Forks High School. The World Health Organization estimates that depression is currently the fourth biggest, most costly, and most disabling illness in the world. It will be the second biggest health problem by 2020 – *in less than ten years*. A shocking fact is that suicide is a leading cause of death among young people in a number of countries. And the most common mental health problem of all is anxiety – one in four people suffer severe anxiety and one in ten people visit a doctor because they feel so tense and stressed (American Foundation for Suicide Prevention, 2011; beyondblue, 2009; Black Dog Institute, 2011; Rey 2000; UK Office for National Statistics, 2011).

It's great that the Twilight Saga describes the psychological experiences of our favorite characters. Even better, the Twilight books point to instructive psychological strategies – really valuable life skills and life-saving skills that will empower you, for life.

## Depression: The Spirit-Sucker

While vampires are called 'blood-suckers' and 'leeches' in the Twilight books, severe depression is much like a 'spirit-sucker' in real life. As Bella's strong feelings of depression suggest, especially in *New Moon*, this condition does seem to suck out a person's inner life force. Just as vampires drink blood, depression greedily drinks all your psychological vitality, draining you of energy. Depression devours your cheerful spirits and your positive thoughts, leaving you feeling weary, wasted and worthless. All the more reason to learn about a stealthy vampiric force that feasts on human happiness. In the Twilight Saga, Bella helps to illustrate important features of depression that will prove most enlightening and empowering.

## Why Is Bella Depressed?

So what causes depression? Why do nice, normal, healthy people – like Bella – become depressed? A stressful time in life can certainly set off depression and sometimes it's caused by a combination of factors working together. Adverse life events (e.g. family conflict, interpersonal conflict, recent loss and disappointment, poor home/school/work conditions) and personal factors (e.g. bad past experiences, personality, brain chemistry, and genetics) can also increase people's chances of developing depression. Sometimes, depression has no obvious cause at all. Since the experience of depression is different for each person, treatment can be tailored to target a person's unique set of symptoms (beyondblue, 2009). The most important thing about depression is that if you *know* something about it, you can increase your personal power to manage it. This makes Bella a very valuable character indeed, because she helps to illustrate depressive features so well.

In Bella's case, which factors might have contributed to her experience of depression? A few factors seem to give rise to her depression in *New Moon*.

## A significant loss

A difficult experience, such as the loss of someone close to you, can lead to depression. Bella has experienced several recent losses. She moved away from her sunny Arizona home and became permanently separated from the care of her mother for the first time. Bella's biggest loss, of course, was when Edward broke up with her. Bella's earlier losses would have made her more prone to depression and then the split with Edward has directly triggered her severe state of depression.

## A stressful event

An accident, attack or abuse can make people more prone to depression. In Bella's case, she's had a fair few of these. She was nearly crushed by a van at school (*Twilight*, p47). Other traumatic events include being brutally attacked and nearly killed by an evil vampire (*Twilight*, p392). Such stressful experiences make people more vulnerable to depression. Although Bella may feel deeply depressed, this does not make her a weak person. What it means is that she has experienced more hardships and horrors than most other people. Most people who have experienced significant stress travel through life OK until a certain event occurs and sets off a depressive episode later in life.

### Early childhood

A tough childhood, such as parents separating, family abuse, domestic violence, or being raised by over-critical and authoritative parents are key factors that contribute to depression. In Bella's case, her parents did separate when she was younger (*Twilight,* p4). Bella's upbringing may have made her more susceptible to feeling depressed and thinking more negatively about the world. In fact, Bella self-reports early on in the series that she is a 'miserable' person with 'depression' (*Twilight,* p60).

### Genetics

A family history of mental illness is another important factor. Conditions like depression run in families. If a person has a parent or a sibling who suffers from depression, that person's odds of becoming depressed are doubled. In Bella's case, there's no evidence to support this factor.

### A physical illness

While illness does not apply to Bella, it's worth noting that Bella has suffered a lot of physical injury. After a violent vampire attacked Bella in a ballet studio, she sustained multiple injuries such as fractured ribs and a broken leg. It took a while for her to recover. These serious physical ailments would increase Bella's chances of becoming depressed.

### Alcohol and drug abuse

This factor definitely increases the risk of depression. However, it does not apply in Bella's case.

***

As you can see, Bella helps to show how certain factors can

increase a person's risk of depression. A few of them have certainly played an active role in Bella's life. Some of these factors may have influenced your own life or the lives of real people you care about and know.

## How Depressed Is Bella?

It's normal to feel sad or miserable at times. But when feelings of sadness become strong, last for a long time, and it becomes hard to cope with daily life, then this may indicate a severe or clinical *depression*. Depression is more than just feeling upset or sad. It's a serious condition that alters your brain chemistry, makes you lose interest in doing things, and stops you from enjoying life (APA, 2005; beyondblue, 2009). In *New Moon*, Bella's depression hits rock-bottom and an all-time low. As Bella shows, depression can become an illness when:

- the mood state is severe
- it lasts for two weeks or more
- it interferes with a person's ability to function at home, school, work or in social situations.

Bella's father was most concerned about Bella isolating herself in her room every day, not 'doing anything', 'moping' around and looking 'lifeless' (*New Moon*, p95).

The good news is that getting the right type of help early makes it much easier for people, just like Bella, to get back on track and deal effectively with depression.

In *New Moon*, Bella illustrates important signs and symptoms of depression. Her features fit with the definition of depression:

- Strong feelings of sadness that last for more than two weeks. In *New Moon*, Bella feels extremely depressed (p84) for several months (p84–92). She is in low spirits and seems lifeless (p95).

- Lowered self-esteem (or self-worth). Bella puts herself down frequently. For example, 'I'm nothing,' she tells herself in *New Moon* (p315).
- Change in sleep patterns in the form of insomnia, broken sleep or excessive sleep. Bella clearly has trouble sleeping because she has nightmares every night (*New Moon*, p122).
- Change in appetite or weight. There's no clear-cut information about Bella's eating habits or weight, so this factor can't be rated for Bella at this time.
- A reduced capacity to experience pleasure. This is when a person shows an inability to enjoy activities, not looking forward to doing things, and a marked drop in hobbies and interests. Bella certainly shows evidence of this crucial depressive feature. She totally withdraws from pleasant and social activities (*New Moon*, p95) and believes she has nothing to look forward to (*New Moon*, p124).
- Impaired concentration and memory, with an increase in negative thinking. Bella keeps going over negative thoughts in her mind. For example: 'It will be as if I'd never existed' (*New Moon*, p84, p123, p124, p125, p160).
- A sense of hopelessness is a significant feature of depression, which Bella shows. She thinks to herself: 'Love, life, meaning . . . over' (*New Moon*, p73). She believes she has no reason to live (*New Moon*, p125) and describes herself as a 'lost moon' with no earth to orbit (*New Moon*, p201).

(Source of symptoms: APA, 2005, Black Dog Institute)

As Bella helps to show, depression is marked by strong feelings of sadness, social withdrawal, and a huge drop in motivation, enjoyment and energy. In fact, Bella describes her severe depression like this: '*I* was changed, my insides altered almost past the point of recognition' (*New Moon*, p124).

If feelings of depression are severe, the symptoms persist

every day for two weeks or longer, and the depression interferes with your ability to cope at home or school or work, then the best thing to do is to make an appointment with your local doctor and seek professional support. I acknowledge that some people, like Bella, worry about seeing a 'shrink' (*New Moon*, p96). However, not getting help can make the depression much worse. In Bella's case, she suffered badly in October, November, December *and* January (*New Moon*, p85–92). I really want to reassure people that there's no need to feel embarrassed or to suffer alone for so long. Depression is a common experience and there are strategies available to help people like Bella master depression and feel better more quickly.

## Mastering Depression

### Reach Out

The best way to deal with a dark psychological force like depression is to reach out and talk to someone about it. Some people think that it's weak to admit that they're going through a really rough time. But if you have depression, you can't just 'snap out of it' or 'pull yourself together'. Talking to someone you trust – like a friend, family member, teacher, or counselor – will help you to feel less isolated and less overwhelmed by the feelings of despair. Make a connection with people you like and who care about you. If you think you are depressed, take action early and reach out for some support (beyondblue, 2009).

An excellent move is to see a doctor or visit a local community health center. Health professionals can give you a proper assessment. They can also show you flashy strategies to help you master your depression. If you or someone you know is feeling suicidal, then it is crucial to get help immediately. I would like to remind all the Bellas, Edwards, Jacobs and other young people out there that depression is a common problem that health professionals know a lot about. These people just want to listen and help.

## Tailored Treatment

Since everyone's depression is different, people can get treatment that matches their individual needs. Some people, for example, will benefit significantly from medical treatments. Antidepressants help to restore any chemical imbalances in the brain. Psychological treatments are especially powerful. An important approach called Cognitive-Behavior Therapy (CBT) teaches people positive skills that will weaken negative thinking and unhelpful behavior patterns. Bella is already using CBT techniques of her own, even if she's not fully aware of it. After spending several months alone in her room, Bella changes her behavior pattern, which helps her to break away from depression:

- Bella starts spending more time with her friend Jacob.
- Bella hangs out in different environments: Jacob's house, a garage, the beach, the forest.
- Bella becomes more active and social: she visits Port Angeles with school friends.
- She engages in new and interesting activities, like learning about motorbikes.

All these actions are CBT-like strategies because they involve: increased physical activity, increased social activity, an increased schedule of pleasant events, and positive distraction techniques. The result? Bella feels much better. Bella's new behavior pattern boosts her feelings of well-being and helps her to break away from a negative soul-sucking force.

## Bella's Negative Thoughts

The way people think significantly influences the way people feel. Since depression involves an increase in negative thinking, this would certainly make feelings of depression worse and more negative too. Bella may not realize it at the time, but her negative thoughts would provoke, strengthen and maintain her depression. In fact, people's thoughts play such a big role in mood that psychologists have developed cognitive famous theories of depression. These include:

### Beck's Cognitive Theory

This theory explains that depressed people think negatively about themselves, the world, and the future. For example, Bella believes: 'I would be the new girl from the big city, a curiosity, a freak . . . I didn't relate well to people' (*Twilight*, p9), which is a negative thought about herself. Adding to this, Bella also thinks 'I detested Forks' (*Twilight*, p4), which is a negative thought about the world. Bella predicts that 'My being happy in Forks is an impossibility' (*Twilight*, p7), which is clearly a negative thought about the future.

### Seligman's Attribution Theory

This theory explains that depressed people blame themselves for failure whilst attributing success to factors outside their personal control. For example, when Edward gets angry, Bella says to him: 'You're angry . . . I shouldn't have said anything' (*Twilight*, p161). In other words, she blames herself for Edward's anger even though she is not responsible for his reactions. Edward is the only one who is in control of his own thoughts and behaviors. Bella's negative thinking style would be aggravating feelings of learned helplessness and depression.

### Ellis's Rational-Emotive Theory

This approach explains that people get depressed because they express irrational beliefs or cognitive distortions. A good example of a major thinking error that produces feelings of depression is called 'labeling'. That's when people give themselves or others negative names. A good Bella example is when she calls herself: 'Stupid, stupid, stupid' (*Twilight*, p57).

That's a negative, negative, negative label, all right.

Since negative thinking plays such an important role in increasing and maintaining depression, the most effective psychological treatments focus on challenging and changing thoughts. A key component of CBT (Cognitive-Behavior Therapy) is 'cognitive restructuring'. This technique shows people how to turn a *negative* thinking style into a more *positive* thinking style.

If we wanted to help someone like Bella decrease her depression, we could target her negative thoughts, challenge them and change them into more positive thoughts:

Negative Thought: Bella, for example, thinks she is 'damaged goods' (*New Moon*, p213).

Cognitive Challenge: What is the evidence?

- What evidence do I have to support my negative thoughts?
- What evidence do I have against them?

This type of questioning helps people to see that the negative thought is unproductive and has no real basis. A more positive thought would be: "No one else has ever called me that – maybe I'm being too self-critical".

Negative Thought: 'I don't trust myself to be . . . enough. To deserve you' (*New Moon*, p523).

Cognitive Challenge: What alternative views are there?

- How might someone else view this situation?
- What is a more helpful way to view this situation?

A more positive idea is: 'I'm sure Jacob would tell me I'm a worthy individual. I do deserve to be happy.'

Negative Thought: 'I'm nothing . . . Nothing special' (*New Moon*, p315).

Cognitive Challenge: How does this thinking affect me?

- Is this thought helping me to feel better, or hindering me from getting what I want? How?

A more realistic way for Bella to think is: 'This thought makes me feel bad. It's better to think of a positive thought to lift my mood such as "I am a smart and caring person".'

Negative Thought: Bella thinks 'He was too perfect. I realized with a piercing stab of despair. There was no way this godlike creature could be meant for me' (*Twilight*, p224).

Cognitive Challenge: What thinking error am I making?

- Am I ignoring shades of grey and all the middle ground? (Black-and-white thinking /All-or-none thinking)

Bella could challenge this thought by thinking something like: 'Hold on, I think this is "all-or-none" thinking. It's unrealistic to think that others are "completely perfect" and that I am "totally flawed".'

Negative Thought: Bella thinks 'Was there anything I touched that didn't get spoiled?' (*Eclipse*, p459).

Cognitive Challenge: Am I making things look much worse than they really are? (catastrophizing)

A more helpful thought for Bella might be: 'Woops! I think I'm exaggerating disaster again.'

Negative Thought: Bella thinks 'If anyone gets hurt, it will always be my fault' (*Eclipse*, p425).

Cognitive Challenge: Am I blaming myself for something that

is not my fault? (personalizing)

To challenge this negative thought, Bella could think: 'That's ridiculous. I don't control bad vampires.'

Negative Thought: Bella thinks, 'My idiocy would not ruin anything else tonight . . . There would be plenty of time to flagellate myself' (*Breaking Dawn*, p63).

Cognitive Challenge: Am I predicting what I think will happen next? (jumping to conclusions)

It appears so. A better thought is: 'I'm expecting myself to wreck everything. This thought is way too negative, so I'll just let it go.'

Negative Thought: Bella thinks, 'I was stupid and slow and human' (*New Moon*, p448).

Cognitive Challenge: Am I focusing on the negatives and ignoring all the good things?

A healthier thought could be: 'How can I be stupid when I've been placed in advanced classes at school? I'm definitely discounting positive evidence here.'

Negative Thought: Bella thinks, 'I'd been broken beyond repair' (*New Moon*, p219).

Cognitive Challenge: What action can I take to improve things?

- What can I do to improve my situation?
- What can I do right now to feel better?
- Who can help me?

A better and more confident thought is: "I've coped before, and I'll find a way to do it again".

(Source of Cognitive Challenge ideas: Powell, 2010)

***

With help from Bella, this important psychological activity shows that anyone can restructure their negative thoughts and reduce feelings of depression. Just as certain factors strengthen depression, other factors and strategies weaken it.

## Suicide: A Total Mental Eclipse

In the Twilight Saga, the darkest and deadliest psychological force of all is suicide. A good visual way to describe suicide is that it is like a total eclipse of the sun. Suicide overshadows all reason and reality. It completely blocks out all hope and happiness. Once strong suicidal urges set in, it is almost impossible to see clearly, think positively, and solve problems. If someone's suicide plans are successful, as Edward's nearly were in Italy, then the result is tragic, destructive and irreversible. As the Twilight books help to show, suicide is a painful and disturbing experience, a full eclipse of the mind, heart, and soul, for sure.

## I Want to Die

In *New Moon,* Edward admits to having had a fully serious 'death-wish'. Edward reveals that he first had suicidal thoughts the year before, when he incorrectly assumed an evil vampire killed Bella. As Edward explains: 'I wasn't going to live without you.' Bella 'didn't want to believe he was serious, but his golden eyes were brooding, focused on something far away in the distance as he contemplated ways to end his own life' (*New Moon,* p19). Later, Edward actually implemented these suicidal plans, after he received some wrong information about Bella.

As you may already know, the Twilight Saga echoes William Shakespeare's play *Romeo and Juliet,* in which two young lovers commit suicide. Both Romeo and Juliet yearned to be together and neither one could live without the other. But the most famous suicidal thoughts ever recorded were from another Shakespeare play called *Hamlet*. Here, a depressed prince contemplates the fatal act:

*To be, or not to be, that is the question:*
*Whether 'tis nobler in the mind to suffer*
*The slings and arrows of outrageous fortune,*
*Or to take arms against a sea of troubles*
*And by opposing end them. To die . . .*

For Prince Hamlet, life is troubling and involves much suffering. And the phrase 'not to be' means taking suicidal action to defy life's painful events.

Edward's suicide attempt in *New Moon* reveals extremely important information about suicide. In particular, his suicide illustrates that being alone when suicidal urges are strong is extremely dangerous. On the upside, Edward's suicide story offers hope. Edward shows that when you're suicidal – and in the company of people who care about you – this can save your life.

## The Fatal Facts

In real life, suicide is almost non-existent in children before adolescence. Then, as soon as young people hit puberty – the age group Bella, Edward, Jacob and their friends belong to – the rate of suicide rises sharply and continues to increase with age. 'Suicidal and self-destructive behaviour is a very worrying development that often appears during adolescence,' says Dr Joseph Rey, who directs adolescent psychiatric services in Sydney. And 'about half of teenagers who attempt suicide once will make further attempts,' he says.

In the United States, someone dies by suicide every 15 minutes. The latest data from the Centers for Disease Control and Prevention reported 34,598 suicides in 2007 – that's a shocking average of 665 suicidal deaths per week. Since not all suicide attempts are officially recorded, it is estimated that almost *one million* people attempt suicide each year in the US. Around 90% of people who committed suicide had a mental illness at the time of their death, often an unrecognized or untreated depression. So not only did people suffer from depression unnecessarily, they could have received help to prevent suicide, just as Edward received help from Bella and Alice in Italy.

As for the United Kingdom, the Office for National Statistics reported 5,675 suicides in 2009 – an average of 109 suicidal deaths each week. Almost three times more males committed suicide than females (4,304 males compared to 1,371 females). During 2000–2009, the highest suicide rates in the UK were among men aged 15–44 years. This means that younger males are at a high risk of suicide. Clearly, too many people are dying in the country that movie star 'Edward' (Robert Pattinson) was born in, and in neighboring nations too.

Did you know that suicide is the biggest cause of death among young people in Australia? The 2010 Australian of the Year and psychiatry professor Patrick McGorry recently reported that suicide 'causes more deaths among young Australians every year than cancer and heart disease combined. Suicide even trumps road accidents, as for every young adult who died on the road another two take their own lives'. The Australian Bureau of Statistics reported 2,098 deaths by suicide in 2004, with almost four times more males dying from suicide than females. So about six people every week took their own lives due to mental and emotional suffering that they could have received help for. As a male aged 15–24 years, this certainly puts Edward (an eternal 17-year-old), and other young people, in a high-risk suicide age bracket.

The best news about suicide is that suicide can be prevented. Not only does Edward raise awareness that too many young people are killing themselves; the Twilight books also allude to powerful suicide prevention techniques.

## Suicide Danger Signs

As Edward shows in his Twilight world, suicidal behavior involves self-injurious thoughts, feelings, plans and actions. Suicide is usually attempted when a person is experiencing a crisis. The most direct and imminent danger signs of suicide include:

- Threatening to hurt or kill oneself
- Looking for ways to kill oneself (weapons, pills, or other lethal methods)
- Talking or writing about death, dying or suicide
- Making plans or preparations for a potentially serious attempt

In *New Moon*, Edward's suicidal behavior embraces all these deadly signs (a threat, a method, a plan, and talking about it). As Bella recalls it:

> *I wasn't going to live without you,* he'd said as watched Romeo and Juliet die . . . *But I wasn't sure how to do it . . . so I was thinking maybe I would go to Italy and do something to provoke the Volturi . . . You don't irritate them unless you want to die.*
> (*New Moon*, p418)

In Edward's case, he certainly was expressing strong suicidal intent and intensity at the time. Alice also noticed that Edward's plans involved 'going to Italy . . . *to die*' (*New Moon*, p417–418).

Other suicide warning signs include:

- Intense anxiety, increased tension, panic attacks
- Feeling desperate or trapped, like there's no way out
- Feeling hopeless
- Feeling there's no reason or purpose to live
- Engaging in reckless or risky activities

- Increased alcohol or drug use
- Expressing violent or self-destructive behavior (like provoking the Volturi)
- Withdrawing from friends or family (Edward went to South America by himself)
- Insomnia (this sign does not apply to Edward, as Twilight vampires don't sleep)

## Let's Assess Risk: How Suicidal Is Edward?

Since suicidal wishes are potentially lethal, it is crucial to assess how serious someone's suicidal wishes are. Some people believe that asking a person about their suicidal ideas may make the person more suicidal. Not true. Encouraging people to talk about suicide usually brings enormous relief. By sharing concerns with someone else, people feel less alone and less overwhelmed by their problems.

To assess suicidal risk, a number of factors must be considered. For example, the planned method of suicide and how lethal it is (e.g. guns, gas, pills). Another important factor is whether other people will be around to see or stop the suicidal act. If someone plans to commit suicide in a remote place, where there are no people around to look out for them, then the risk of a successful suicide is much higher.

## Hopelessness – The Best Predictor

The best predictor of suicide is a sense of hopelessness. The stronger the feelings of hopelessness, the higher the risk of suicide. People who feel hopeless are in so much mental distress that they believe suicide is the only way to escape their pain. A person who feels hopeless may say things like 'I just want to end it all', 'There's no other solution', 'I can't stand these awful feelings anymore', or 'Things will never get better.'

Since hopelessness determines suicide attempts and completions, one of the best things to do is to increase a person's feelings of hope and personal control. This will help to reduce the risk of suicide considerably.

In Edward's situation, examples of hopeless ideas he probably had in his mind:

- 'There is no point to living; Bella is gone forever.'
- 'I can't stand life now that Bella is dead. I can never be happy again.'
- 'I feel so lost and alone and miserable. Killing myself is the way out.'

These kinds of statements convey a strong sense of hopelessness – feeling trapped in a bad or unbearable situation from which there is no escape.

To boost your suicide-spotting skills, check out Edward's suicide risk-assessment below. Not only will this help you to understand just how depressed and hopeless Edward may have been feeling in *New Moon*, you will gain some knowledge and skills in the assessment of suicidal behavior. One day, these skills may prove radically useful for you, your friends, or other people you care about in real life. So let's do a suicide risk-assessment on a vampire, by checking out which suicide risk factors apply to Edward.

| **Significant Suicide Risk Factors** | **Yes** | **No** | **Not Known** | **What's the evidence for Edward?** |
|---|---|---|---|---|
| Expressing Suicidal Ideas | ✓ | | | Edward clearly intends to commit suicide. He has gone to Italy to die (*New Moon*, p417). |
| History of Suicidal Attempts and Behaviour | ✓ | | | 1) Edward has considered suicide before, when he believed an evil vampire killed Bella (*New Moon*, p18-19).<br>2) Edward has asked the Volturi vampires to kill him (*New Moon*, p433). |
| Has a Suicide Plan | ✓ | | | Edward has a plan to provoke the Volturi to kill him, by stepping into the sun. The Volturi kill those who reveal themselves as vampires (*New Moon*, 438). Edward's plan is very detailed, which increases his suicide risk drastically:<br>The <u>date</u> is planned – Saint Marcus Day, which celebrates the purging of vampires (*New Moon*, p440).<br>The <u>time</u> is set – noon (*New Moon*, p441).<br>The <u>place</u> is arranged – under the clock tower in the city plaza (*New Moon*, 439). |
| **Other Risk Factors** | **Yes** | **No** | **Not Known** | **Evidence for Edward?** |
| Major psychiatric diagnosis | | | ✓ | There's not enough information to assess this factor for Edward. |
| Symptoms of depression | ✓ | | | Edward shows some clear signs of depression. He withdrew from his family, isolated himself in South America, and has made firm suicide plans (*New Moon*, p399, p418). |
| History using drugs/alcohol | | ✓ | | Not part of Edward's vampire diet. |

| | | | | |
|---|---|---|---|---|
| High level of distress | ✓ | | | To rate this factor accurately it would be best to talk to Edward. It is noted that Edward is not communicating with anyone and that he keeps changing his mind all the time. |
| Feeling hopeless/help less | ✓ | | | Edward feels hopeless because he believes Bella is dead. Her death is something he is helpless to control. |
| History of self-harm behaviours without suicidal intent | | | ✓ | There's no information to suggest that Edward has ever hurt himself deliberately (like cutting himself or burning himself) |
| Impulsivity; unstable mental state | ✓ | | | "He keeps changing his mind" (*New Moon*, p425); "Chaotic... flickers... he was changing his plans so quickly" (*New Moon* p437). This shows that Edward's state of mind is very unsettled. |
| Recent stress or loss – death, relationship breakup, work/retiring, finances, accommodation | ✓ | | | Edward recently broke up with Bella against his wishes. He believed this would keep her safe (*New Moon*, p68). |
| Lack of social support | | ✓ | | Edward travelled alone to carry out his secret suicide plan. Fortunately, Alice "saw" he went to Italy so she and Bella followed him to help. This social support increases Edward's safety because the girls plan to stop him (*New Moon*, p438). |

(**Source of Risk Factors**: Queensland Government, 2011; Manual of Mental Health Care in General Practice, 2000)

As you can see, Edward has a fair few suicide risk factors. Most importantly, this includes all three 'significant' risk factors at the start of the checklist: 1) suicidal ideas, 2) suicide history, and 3) suicide plans. The more 'YES' factors there are, the higher the risk of someone committing suicide. As a result, the need to talk to a doctor, nurse, parent, teacher or friend is much more urgent and important. Anyone who is feeling suicidal needs to seek support immediately.

While formal suicide risk-assessments are done by qualified health professionals, this sample assessment on Edward will have enhanced your awareness about suicidal behavior considerably. What's more, there are powerful ways to reduce suicidal suffering and help yourself (or someone else) survive suicide.

## Suicide Survival Skills

There are powerful techniques that people can use to help themselves or others survive suicide. Suicidal thoughts play terrible tricks on a person's mind, like convincing people that their problems cannot be fixed, or that the future will never improve, or that there's no light at the end of a dark tunnel. If you know how suicidal thoughts work, however, you can increase your chances of surviving a serious emotional crisis. If you, or someone you know, are feeling suicidal, here are some things you can do to prevent suicide. You don't even need a bright yellow Porsche 911 Turbo to be a flashy psychological rescue machine.

## Get Good Support

If you (or someone you care about) is threatening suicide, thinking about dying, or making suicide plans, these are signs of an acute crisis. Such warning signs must be taken seriously. Things you can do to survive suicide:

- If someone tells you they are feeling suicidal, tell the person you are concerned.
- Let the person know you care, that he/she is not alone, and that the suicidal urges fade after a while.
- Do not leave the person alone.
- Ask whether the person has developed a specific suicide plan or method.

- Find out if the person has a doctor or is taking medication.
- Don't say things like 'You have a lot to live for' or 'Your suicide will hurt people close to you'. This could make the person feel worse.
- If safe, remove any guns, drugs or sharp objects that could be used for suicide.
- Take the person to the emergency section of your nearest hospital, health clinic, or mental health center.
- If the above options are not available, call an emergency number or a suicide hotline.

It is really important to stay with a suicidal person, if safe and possible. If a mentally unstable person is left alone – even if it's just for a moment – this gives the person a complete opportunity to get away and kill themselves. If you're feeling suicidal, the best thing to do is to be with someone. Go somewhere where there are people – a friend's place, a drop-in center, a local health service.

People who contemplate suicide often don't believe they can be helped, so you may need to actively assist a suicidal person to get help or see a qualified health professional. For example, just before Edward planned to walk out into the midday sun in Volterra, Italy, he seemed to be in a depressed daze: 'Edward stood motionless as a statue . . . His expression was very peaceful, like he was dreaming pleasant things' (*New Moon*, p451). At that particular moment, Edward did not have the ability to stop himself. Bella grabbed him just in time.

As the Twilight Saga shows, getting good support – like being in the company of people who care, talking to someone you like and trust – goes a long way, and maybe all the way, to stop suicide.

(Source: American Foundation for Suicide Prevention, 2011)

## Ride the Waves

In people's personal experience, suicidal urges tend to come and go in waves. These waves usually peak and pass after a few hours. In this case, an excellent way to outsmart suicide is to *delay* suicidal urges and ride out the suicidal waves. Here's some helpful information from Aussie GP Dr Simon Bridge to help you survive suicidal thoughts:

- The thoughts isolate you: they discourage you from telling other people that you are suffering.
- Strong suicidal thoughts trick you into thinking that your friends and family are better off without you, and that you have no future. This is not true.
- People rarely suicide in company. If you start to feel really suicidal, be with someone.
- Alcohol and drugs feed suicidal thoughts and make you feel worse.
- The strong feelings of depression will pass and the negative thoughts will eventually lose their grip on you.

(Source: www.kirinaran.com)

If someone like Edward is feeling really suicidal, he could delay his suicidal activities. For example, by staying away from the clock tower at midday to allow his death-wish to fade. Or ringing Alice on his mobile phone. Eventually, Edward's suicidal urges will diminish and disappear. Even the leader of the Volturi vampires pointed this out:

> 'You see, Edward?' The strange vampire turned and smiled at Edward like a fond but scolding grandfather.
>
> 'What did I tell you? Aren't you glad that I didn't give you what you wanted yesterday?'
>
> 'Yes, Aro. I am,' he agreed.
>
> (*New Moon*, p468)

Edward had a strong urge to kill himself just hours earlier, but this urge has now passed. Edward's circumstances have changed and he no longer feels so suicidal. Hopefully, if Edward ever feels suicidal again, he will delay his urges and outsmart those sneaky suicidal thoughts.

### Reasons to Live

Mental health experts use a number of powerful techniques to help suicidal people. According to psychologists at the Oxford Cognitive Therapy Centre in the United Kingdom, a really effective suicide crisis intervention strategy is to get the person to postpone suicide and rethink suicide as an option. This may involve:

- Encouraging the person to think about the pros/cons of living and dying
- Promoting reasons for living
- Reinforcing the disadvantages of dying
- Identifying deterrents to suicide (What would stop/deter you from committing suicide?)
- Forward time projection (What would happen to people who care about you if you died?)
- Asking 'What if you were wrong?' (that suicide is the only solution)
- Problem-solving

(Source: Bennett-Levy, 2009)

To help decrease Edward's feelings of suicide, a useful and popular technique would be to ask Edward to list his 'Top 10 Reasons for Living'. Edward's reasons for existing might be:

1 I love my family.
2 Killing myself will hurt those who care about me.
3 It's unlikely my misery will be eternal. But suicide is forever.

4 Things will get better; they always do.
5 There are things in the world that I would still like to experience.
6 I want to travel to interesting places.
7 I might get passionate about a career, just like my dad loves medicine.
8 I could do something fulfilling, like protecting endangered animals.
9 I really enjoy playing baseball during thunderstorms.
10 I love composing classical music.

As you can see, Edward's 'Top 10 Reasons to Live' makes suicidal look a lot less desirable. Such a list also helps to show that the damage caused by suicide (e.g. hurting others; suicide is forever) is significant and permanent, whilst a miserable mood passes (e.g. things will get better). This suicide-intervention technique helps suicidal people feel a lot less 'trapped'. It is very successful with all kinds of suicidal people who feel stuck in a bad situation or have trouble thinking positively, clearly, or flexibly.

## Anxiety: A Hungry Hunter

### Does Bella Have Anxiety?

Anxiety is like a hungry hunter. It is a restless force that tries to stalk you, spook you, follow you, feed on you, bring you down, wind you up, and wear you out. Anxiety is prevalent in Bella's life and it is the most common mental health problem of all in real life. While some anxiety is productive and necessary for survival, excessive anxiety levels are harmful to health and well-being.

In the Twilight Saga, Bella shows many symptoms of anxiety. While it's normal for everyone to feel anxious from time to time, overwhelming anxiety that cannot be easily controlled is called an *anxiety disorder*. It's much more than just feeling stressed – it's a serious condition that makes daily life difficult to cope with. At worst, extreme anxiety can take the form of phobias and panic attacks, crippling and paralyzing people with strong feelings of fear (beyondblue, 2009). If people like Bella don't want their anxiety to get worse, it's best to get informed about this prowling predator.

## The Anxiety Experience

In the Twilight books, Bella shows recurring signs of anxiety. At times, her anxiety seems quite strong. It's hard to tell if Bella has an anxiety disorder though, without a proper interview with her. But she does seem to show some major symptoms.

So, what causes anxiety disorders? Well, a family history of mental health problems, stressful life events, an ongoing physical illness, and personality factors contribute to anxiety. Bella's background certainly fits with these factors – her parents separated when she was a child and Bella's sensitive personality compels her to worry a lot about others. Bella has also experienced stressful incidents in the past, like vampire attacks and a van nearly crushing her at school.

In the Twilight series, Bella helps to illustrate all three parts of the anxiety experience. Anxiety symptoms affecting the body, behavior, and thoughts, that is.

## Body

When people are anxious – in real danger or believe they are being threatened – the body releases adrenaline. This energizes the body to fight or flee the threat in these ways.

### Heart races

This happens in order to pump more blood around the body so that people can fight better or run faster. Bella examples:

- 'My heart throbbed' (*Twilight*, p183).
- Bella feels her 'pulse hammering' through her veins (*Twilight*, p243).

## Breathing quickens

This works to provide more oxygen to the lungs and the bloodstream, and improve strength. It may also cause irregular breathing, choking, breathlessness, chest pain, and dizziness. Bella examples:

- 'I felt my breathing gradually creeping towards hyperventilation' (*Twilight*, p13).
- Bella was 'feeling dizzy' (*Twilight*, p192).

## Muscles tense

This prepares the body for action. But it can also cause tension, aches, shaking or trembling. Bella examples:

- 'I cringed' (Twilight, p22).
- '"H-how do you know my name?" I stammered' (*Twilight*, p37).
- 'My throat suddenly felt tight' (*Twilight*, p47).
- 'My hands started to shake' (*Twilight*, p62).
- 'I leaned back, stunned . . . frightened by his reaction' (*Twilight*, p189).
- 'I fought back a shiver' (*Twilight*, p189).
- 'The bell rang loudly, making me jump' (*Twilight*, p21).
- 'My left hand clenched into a fist' (*Eclipse*, p406).

## Digestion shutdown

Since the heart and muscles need more energy, the digestive system slows down to save on energy. This may cause nausea, stomach churning, and dry mouth. Bella example:

- 'I sipped my soda slowly, my stomach churning' (*Twilight*, p35).

**Sweating**

Sweat and blood capillaries rise to the skin's surface to cool down the body and stop the muscles from overheating. A side effect is blushing. Bella examples:

- 'I looked down, flushing' (*Twilight*, p148).
- 'I stammered, blushed, and tripped over' (*Twilight*, p15).

**Pupils dilate**

During anxiety, the pupils enlarge to improve vision. Bella examples:

- '"Bella, what are you staring at?" Jessica intruded, her eyes following my stare' (*Twilight*, p35).
- 'Face ashen, eyes wide, I sat like a bird locked in the eyes of a snake' (*Twilight*, p232).

**Behavior**

Anxiety also affects behavior. People who experience strong anxiety often behave in ways to minimize contact with the things they fear. In the Twilight books, Bella provides some classic examples of anxious behavior:

**Avoidance**

This includes avoiding people or places, not going into situations you fear. Good Bella example:

- 'If he was glaring at me, I would skip Biology, like the coward I was' (*Twilight*, p35).

**Escape**

This might involve escaping quickly, leaving situations as early as possible. Bella example:

- 'I waved briefly . . . and then shut the door before they were gone' (*Twilight*, p309).

## Safety behaviors

These are unhelpful coping behaviors that people use to decrease feelings of anxiety. Such behaviors include drinking alcohol, smoking cigarettes, taking medication, fiddling with clothes or objects, avoiding eye contact, and always having a 'lucky charm' on you. A few classic Bella examples:

- 'I cut the engine as soon as I was in a spot, so that the thunderous volume wouldn't draw attention to me' (*Twilight*, p13).
- 'I let my hair fall over my right shoulder, making a dark curtain between us' (*Twilight*, p21).
- 'I dropped my head, letting my hair fall to conceal my face' (*Twilight*, p35).
- 'Cowardly as ever, I shifted my hair over my right shoulder to hide my face' (*Twilight*, p63).
- 'I looked away before I could start hyperventilating' (*Twilight*, p192).
- 'I looked down . . . I kept my eyes down on the table' (*Twilight*, p183).

Judging by the versatility of Bella's behavior pattern, she is a bit of a female 'Houdini', skilled in the artistry of avoidance. However, avoidance, escape, and safety behaviors will only make the anxiety worse because people never get a chance to find out that they *can* cope with situations less anxiously without using all the safety tricks.

## Thoughts

People who experience strong anxiety excel at worry. They are also good at overestimating the actual amount of danger involved in a situation. Anxious people are also good at putting themselves down and minimizing their ability to cope. Some typical thoughts that anxiety sufferers think are:

- 'I'm in danger right now.'
- 'The worst possible things will happen.'
- 'What if I can't cope?'
- 'I don't think I can handle it.'

Some obvious examples of Bella thinking anxiously:

- 'I went through different arguments . . . in my head' (*Twilight*, p14).
- 'I'd been plagued by a persistent, uncomfortable intrusion of a specific mental picture. It popped into my thoughts at regular intervals like some annoying alarm clock' (*Eclipse*, p34).
- 'It was a hundred times worse than I imagined' (*New Moon*, p25).
- 'What if the time had run out? What if Jacob and Edward got too close? What if Edward decided to join in the fight? The icy fear pooled in my stomach' (*Eclipse*, p461).

***

As Bella helps to show quite well, anxiety influences the 'body', 'behavior', and 'thoughts'. What's more, these three symptom areas are all interlocked in a vicious cycle.

## The Anxiety Cycle

Anxiety symptoms influence each other. They provoke and aggravate each other. They are closely interrelated. A worry, for example, might activate a physical symptom that worsens the worry. The worse worry, in turn, may make the physical symptoms stronger. This builds up to a point where a person will want to make a fast get-away from a situation that provokes anxiety. Alternatively, a person might try to avoid certain situations altogether. In psychology, this is called *the anxiety cycle.*

## Bella's Prom Night

Consider Bella's reactions to the school prom. We already know she feels nervous in the social spotlight and that she worries about looking awkward dancing in front of others. So an anxiety-provoking situation for Bella might be a guy asking her to go to the school prom. This situation might trigger an anxious thought like: 'Maybe something bad will happen to me.' Bella's anxious thought could evoke physical anxiety symptoms: she might start blushing, sweating, or feeling sick. These physical sensations may cause Bella to worry even more: 'I'll have a terrible time', 'I will look really stupid', 'I'll blush so badly that everyone will stare at me.' Such symptoms, which spur each other on, may make Bella's anxiety so strong that she will try to avoid the prom altogether. In fact, this is exactly what happens.

In *Twilight,* Bella tells Edward about her scheme to avoid the school prom: 'I would have cancelled later – faked an illness or a sprained ankle' (*Twilight,* p185). Why? Not because she's a callous and manipulative liar. It's because of her high anxiety. Bella is so 'freaked out' about looking clumsy ('You've never seen me in Gym, I guess' – *Twilight,* p186) that she will do just about anything to avoid drawing attention to herself. But avoiding the school dance will only increase Bella's anxiety further. Like a hungry hunter, Bella's anxiety would eat away at her happiness and gobble up all her self-confidence. In which case, it's good that Bella did attend the prom. Bella showed that she's the boss, not her anxiety. She also found she enjoyed it more than she 'predicted' and that she had a nice time dancing with Edward, after all. At a graduation party the following year, which Bella attended, she again noticed that: 'It wasn't as hard as I'd thought it would be' (*Eclipse,* p327).

## Taming Anxiety

What are some of the best things someone like Bella can do to reduce anxiety? What are the most effective psychological techniques to tame anxiety? Can anxiety disorders be treated? Fortunately, there are highly helpful ways to manage anxiety. Some psychological techniques, in particular, are pretty effective. With help from the Twilight books, here are three sure-fire ways to tame anxiety.

## Track the Triggers

To decrease feelings of anxiety, one of the best moves to make first is to identify triggers. In other words, know what sort of things make you feel anxious in the first place. When are the times when you are more likely to get anxious? In what situations? Who with? If you can uncover the patterns, then you can plan ahead, do something new to break the anxiety cycle, and prepare yourself to deal effectively with those situations. Possible triggers could be:

- Certain places, e.g. 'The forest around Forks freaks me out.'
- Certain people, e.g. 'I like vegetarian vampires, but those Volturi are pretty creepy.'
- Certain times, e.g. 'I think I'm more scared of vampires after dark.'
- Thinking ahead about things, e.g. 'There's no way I'll go grocery shopping unless I have a backpack full of wooden stakes and silver bullets – you never know who you could bump into in the chocolate aisle.'

Maybe you have a certain anxiety pattern. By tracking down the triggers, you're gathering information that will help you design an appropriate anxiety-busting plan that suits *your* needs. You can then select strategies ahead of time that work for you or practice special anxiety-busting skills beforehand that target the things that make you anxious. If the Forks forest freaks you out at night, for example, you can go for early evening walks with a friend, until your anxiety about the forest subsides. Then, to reduce your anxiety further, you could try going for walks with a nice werewolf. Later, when you feel even more confident, you can take short walks alone, and reduce your feelings of anxiety about the forest *gradually over time.*

## Positive Self-Talk

Since anxious thoughts boost anxiety, it makes sound sense to address the anxious thoughts. One psychological technique is called positive self-talk. This simply involves swapping negative thoughts with positive thoughts.

In *Breaking Dawn,* it's the dawn of positive self-talk for Bella. Her thinking style becomes less negative and much more positive overall. For example:

- To stop worrying about her upcoming wedding, Bella tells herself: 'I was with Edward in my happy place' (*Breaking Dawn,* p20). She replaces her worry with a positive thought.
- When Bella starts to worry about being in the social spotlight at her wedding, she tells herself: 'I just had to get over myself. Attention was an inevitable part of life' (*Breaking Dawn,* p28). Bella swaps a negative thought with a more realistic positive thought.
- Just before taking a moonlight swim with Edward on her wedding night, Bella tells herself: 'Don't be a coward' (*Breaking Dawn,* p76). And she wasn't.

The three simple steps to positive self-talk are:

### 1. Check the thoughts

Next time you feel anxious, make a note of the thoughts you are thinking at the time. A good idea is to write thoughts down on a small notepad, as they occur. This way, you 'catch' the thoughts that are setting off your anxiety.

### 2. Challenge the thoughts

People's thoughts become distorted under stress. It is therefore helpful to check the thoughts to see if they are overly negative or unrealistic. If Bella starts feeling anxious, she can ask herself questions like:

- 'Am I looking at this too negatively?'
- 'Am I putting too much pressure on myself?'
- 'Is there a better way to look at this?'
- 'What advice would I give someone else in the same situation?'
- 'What are the most helpful things to think and do in this case?'

### 3. Change the thoughts

The last step simply involves replacing an anxious thought with a calm thought. Reword a distorted negative thought with a more realistic and positive one. For example, when Bella gets out of her old red truck on the first day of school at Forks, she tells herself: 'I can do this' (*Twilight*, p13). That's positive self-talk in action.

Some other positive self-statements people can use to tame anxiety include:

- 'It's not going to be as bad as I think.'
- 'If I do get bad feelings, I know they won't last long and I can cope with them.'
- 'I might enjoy it if I go.'
- 'I'll just concentrate on what I have to do now.'
- 'One step at a time.'
- 'Relax and think positive.'

- 'I coped well with that – great!'
- 'I handled that; it will be easier next time.'
- 'I am pleased with the progress I have made.'

(Source of ideas: Powell, 2010)

Twilight's Bella helps to illustrate some important psychological techniques to decrease anxiety. As Bella shows, the power of positive self-talk soothes anxiety and makes weddings and honeymoons much more pleasant and enjoyable.

## Defuse Loaded Thoughts

Defusing loaded thoughts, much like a bomb expert defuses armed bombs, basically involves removing a thought's emotional charge. Defusion is so easy that people don't even have to fight, challenge, or change their negative (depressed or anxious) thoughts. They just let their thoughts rise, fall, and flow through their minds naturally. Imagine that an anxious thought or worry has just arrived in Bella's mind. What can she do to reduce her anxiety? Answer: Distance herself from the thought and *defuse* it:

1. Notice the thought – just notice that a thought has appeared in your mind.
2. Observe the thought neutrally – don't react emotionally, just be aware that the thought is there.
3. Focus on the present – focus on what you're supposed to be doing or on something helpful. If your mind wanders off to your worries again, just let the worry go and redirect your attention to the present again or to your immediate task. Do this as often as you need to.

(Source: Centre for Clinical Interventions, 2011)

Just noticing or 'acknowledging the thought as a thought, not reacting automatically, and then choosing to put our focus of attention elsewhere' decreases anxiety dramatically, says the UK

GET Self-Help website. For example, Alice uses 'cognitive defusion' to reduce Bella's anxiety on her wedding day:

- 'Go to your happy face, Bella. It won't take long.'
- I sucked in a deep breath and closed my eyes.

(*Breaking Dawn*, p18)

As we defuse upsetting emotional thoughts, they have less and less impact and influence over us. Dr Russell Harris, a doctor and psychotherapist, explains that people can defuse unpleasant thoughts as creatively as they want to. For example, you can:

- Simply observe the thought coolly and unemotionally
- Repeat the thought over and over out loud until it becomes a meaningless sound
- Imagine the thought spoken in a silly voice
- Sing the thought in tune to happy songs
- Put the phrase: 'This is a thought about . . .' in front of the negative thought, to remind yourself that it is only a *thought*, not a *fact*.

Get it? By defusing thoughts (cognitive defusion) you 'distance' yourself from the negative emotional energy of the thought, which makes it bother you less. You're defusing or weakening the importance you might normally attach to the troubling thought too. Just think, you're not even trying to challenge or change negative thoughts, *just seeing the thoughts as thoughts*. Thoughts are simply pieces of language, images, and words. Why try to scare yourself with your own thoughts?

## The Thunderbird's Gift

The Native American Quileute people, who feature in the Twilight series, have something wise and valuable to say about psychological suffering. As an ancient legend tells it, the Quileute people were once very sad and suffered much a long, long time ago. A strong winter storm badly battered the lands. Large hailstones killed people and destroyed a lot of crops. Meanwhile, the rivers of ice and stormy seas prevented people from fishing. The Quileute community were so hungry that people started to die.

Eventually, the Great Chief called a meeting. 'Take comfort,' the wise old Chief told his community. 'We will ask the Great Spirit for help.' So the Chief summoned the Spirit while his people watched and waited in their cold, dark, and silent world.

All of a sudden, a loud noise and flashes of lightning appeared in the sky. A giant bird, with fiery eyes and whirring wings, flew towards the starving people. In its claws the creature held a huge whale, which it placed on the ground. Then, the great Thunderbird flew back into the sky, back into the setting sun, back to the Spirit's hunting grounds perhaps. The Thunderbird brought food, which saved the Quileute people from starving to death.

To this day, the Quileute people know that the Great Spirit can hear them. And their tale shares this important psychological wisdom:

- The world can be a cold, stormy and dark place at times. This can give rise to dark psychological forces like depression, anxiety and hopelessness.
- Without essential nourishment – food, water, positive beliefs, spiritual ideas – your world can look bleak and you might not survive strong despair.
- No matter how bad things get, never give up – believe in yourself, follow your heart, and look to higher forces. Keep spiritual power alive.
- When you take positive psychological action – even if it's just a prayer, spell, poem, or positive affirmation – this can ignite great change.

- Even if you think that you will die because things seem so bad, or you want to die because you're suffering too much psychological pain, always remember this: It's from the dark storm – in some grand form – that hope will fly out, making your spirit fly high and free.

The Thunderbird's gift was a whale. But its greatest gift was a psychological one: hope.

# 6

# I Choose: Bella's Quest for Happiness

*What do you want most in life? For most of us, the answer is 'to be happy'. In a survey of more than 10,000 people from 48 countries, happiness was viewed as more important than success, intelligence, knowledge, maturity, wisdom, relationships, wealth, and meaning in life.*

- Todd Kashdan, psychology professor

## Positive Psychology Shines

### Twilight's Positive Psychology

Every character in the Twilight Saga is on a personal mission. Bella and Edward pursue love. Jacob is exploring his new identity as a teen wolf. Carlisle delights in healing others. Esme enjoys supporting her family. Renee travels and Charlie works. Despite very different goals, every character is, in fact, on the same quest: to find happiness. As a result, the Twilight world introduces a new area of psychology called *positive psychology*. The 2000 founder of the positive psychology movement, Dr Martin Seligman, describes positive psychology much like an exciting quest in that it 'takes you through the countryside of pleasure and gratification, up into the high country of strength and virtue, and finally to the peaks of lasting fulfillment: meaning and purpose'.

Positive psychology explores the positive side of human life – happiness, personal strengths, psychological well-being, and optimal emotional experiences. Best of all, Twilight Saga characters demonstrate some of the best-kept secrets about happiness in line with the psychological literature. Adventures in the Twilight Saga, especially Bella's quest for happiness, shine with ideas from positive psychology.

## Happiness: Fast Facts

What is happiness? How much power do we have to increase our happiness? Do some strategies work better than others? Which characters in the Twilight Saga experience authentic happiness? To most people, the idea of happiness relates to elated feelings like joy, cheerfulness, or contentment. For centuries, philosophers, mystics and writers have scrutinized happiness and the best ways to achieve it. Now, scientists and psychologists have joined the quest to understand happiness and how positive emotions work.

In particular, positive psychology is keen to identify those factors and conditions that help people to thrive, flourish, and be happy.

Some important factors associated with happiness include:

- Making a contribution to society, e.g. Charlie has a police career, Billy Black is a Quileute council elder
- Mixing and expanding socially, e.g. enemies become allies once Jacob joins the Cullens to protect innocent lives
- Developing positive relationships with others, e.g. Bella strives to get along with everyone; she is 'neutral country. I am Switzerland' (*Eclipse*, p128)

If the quest for true happiness is successful, then the benefits are much bigger than the obvious feel-good factor. According to Barbara Fredrickson from the University of Michigan, positive feelings have 'a grand purpose in evolution. Positive emotional mind sets widen our range of thoughts and actions, fostering play, exploration and creativity'. What this means is that the experience of happiness empowers people to:

- Solve problems better
- Think more creatively and laterally
- Be more open to new ideas and new experiences
- Develop valuable survival resources such as tools, knowledge, or social alliances

Later, when times are tough – like if an army of Volturi vampires drops in to execute you – individuals and groups can turn to their resilient inner resources to boost survival and success.

## Twilight's Best Happiness Secret

The Twilight series illustrates some of the most important factors that determine happiness. Bella's quest for happiness reveals the best and most powerful secret of all. A special strategy that not only provides insight into how she achieves happiness, but is also strongly supported by research evidence in psychology, is readily available to everyone, and you can use it to empower your own life.

## Make Powerful Choices

> 'Just because we've been dealt a certain hand . . . it doesn't mean that we can't choose to rise above – to conquer the boundaries of destiny that none of us wanted' (*Twilight*, p268).

Exactly! Edward's comment above reveals one of the most important findings in the science of happiness: *happiness is largely determined by choice*. In the study of happiness, psychologists have found that:

- About 50% of people's happiness is due to *genetics*. For example, researcher Dr David Lykken from the University of Minnesota found evidence to support the role of biological factors when he studied hundreds of sets of twins. Even if twins had different life experiences or were raised apart, genes still accounted for about half of a person's happiness.

- Less than 10% of happiness is influenced by *demographics* and the *environment* – which is age, sex, race, and life circumstances altogether. An overwhelming amount of psychology research has conclusively shown that things like education, marriage, occupation, and income don't increase happiness by much at all. In fact, world well-being expert Professor Ed Diener from the University of Illinois interviewed the richest Americans from the Forbes 400 list. What he found was that extremely wealthy individuals were only 'slightly' happier than everybody else.
- The single biggest factor that determines our happiness is *thought* – how we choose to think. Our personal thoughts, attitudes, and choices determine a whopping 40% of our happiness (Lubomirsky, 2007).

If we could explain happiness as a simple mathematical formula, happiness could be stated like this:

Happiness = 50% Genetics + 10% Environment + *40% Choice*

This means that regardless of who you are biologically and your life circumstances right now, you have the power to increase your happiness levels significantly.

In line with positive psychology research, that is precisely the Twilight Saga's powerful message about happiness. Dr Cullen, for example, did not 'choose' to be a vampire. Life circumstances outside of his control turned him into one after he was attacked. So how does Carlisle cope with this significant life event? By choosing to deal with his new circumstances in the most positive way possible. As Carlisle explains to Bella: 'Like everything in life, I just had to decide what to do with what I was given' (*New Moon*, p35).

What Dr Cullen means is that we can't change the things that have happened to us, but we can choose our reactions to them. We can make the most of what we have. We can acknowledge the positives and appreciate the good things. We can choose to be happy. Choice changes our experiences. Choice conquers chance.

The world renowned psychiatrist Dr William Glasser revolutionized health, education, other human service settings, and many individual lives with a famous approach he called 'choice theory'. This theory's main premise is that: *We almost always have choices, and the better the choice, the more we will be in control of our lives.*

In his best-selling book *Man's Search for Meaning*, the eminent European psychiatrist Dr Victor Frankl has the same view: 'Everything can be taken from a person but one thing: the last of the human freedoms – to choose one's attitude in any given set of circumstances, to choose one's own way.'

If you don't like your current experience, you can make choices to change, adapt, and improve your experience positively and constructively. Alice points this out in *Twilight*: 'The future isn't set in stone. Things change' (p253). Her comment fits well with the most empowering views and findings in psychology – that positive choices create a positive destiny. You can create a better future.

There are many signs in the Twilight Saga to suggest that Bella's ending should have been miserable. Bella admitted to feeling depressed at the very start of *Twilight*. Bella was not living with happily married parents and each parent has been struggling with their own personal issues. Then, in *New Moon*, she experienced a severe episode of depression after Edward broke up with her. She almost killed herself jumping off a cliff (*New Moon*), not to mention a series of near-death experiences from evil vampire attacks in all four books. Does this mean that people like Bella are doomed to be failures in life? Miserable forever? No way. As the science of happiness proves, positive choices exert a significant influence on people's lives. The way people think about things helps them to rise above their biological conditions and outside settings and setbacks.

Consider Bella's choices. Once Bella chooses to be with Edward, her immediate physical and psychological health improves immensely in a number of ways. For example, Bella:

- Feels 'euphoric' (p269)
- Expresses emotions more easily (p273)
- Feels happy and 'rejoices' (p273)
- Shows strong 'enthusiasm' (p273)
- Appears to have brighter eyes (p274)
- Half-runs around the house (p274)
- Reports being in a happy mood (p275)
- Views the world positively: the 'kitchen was bright, happy' (p275)
- Sleeps better (p275)
- Shows a healthy appetite (p276)
- 'Laughs' with Edward (p240)
- Makes jokes (p275)
- Smiles (p269)
- Shows playful behavior (p275)

(*Twilight*)

In *New Moon*, Bella maintains her happiness high. She describes her relationship with Edward as an unbelievable 'degree of good fortune' (*New Moon*, p7). Bella's choice to be with Edward produces strong feelings of happiness.

Bella illustrates that people who believe that they have a fair amount of personal control over their lives are much happier, healthier and more successful than people who believe outside forces determine fate. To achieve *true* happiness, the first step is to be aware that you can make positive choices that work well in your favor.

## My True Place: Bella's Shiny Choices

'You're a completely different person than I am. You make your own kinds of mistakes' (*Breaking Dawn*, p16).

When Bella is deciding whether or not to marry Edward, her mother encourages her to make her own decision. Everyone is different. Different things make different people happy. Since the most important quest of all in life is to be happy, it is all the more important to explore your inner self deeply to make sure that your choices support the things that matter most to you.

Edward may not be Mr Right for you, but for Bella, choosing Edward satisfies a number of her previously unmet needs. With two emotionally distant parents and no other family on the scene, it makes sound psychological sense for Bella to pick a partner like Edward. He is above average affection-wise, protective, and a real romantic. Edward therefore gives Bella the love she never had. He makes her life feel more fulfilling and whole. A less wise choice of partner for Bella might be a career-crazy guy – a copy of her career-driven dad. But no, Bella did not choose a sleazy human schoolboy, a replica of her father, nor did she become a member of the uncaring Volturi clan (even though Aro, ever so sweetly, invited her to). Rather, Bella chose to be with someone who adores her, dotes on her, and lavishes every affection on her. Sure, no character, real or fictional – not even Edward – is perfect or without psychological flaws. But Bella's choice proves positive and is the best possible choice for *her*. Above all, it makes her feel good: 'I. Am. Happy' (*Breaking Dawn*, p83).

## Bella Blooms

In the first Twilight book, there's a really amazing and well-hidden psychological adventure in the forest. It captures the moment when Bella's choice to be with Edward becomes clear and her happiness starts to bloom. Bella is hiking though the forest, weaving her way easily through a green maze thick with trees (which is a pretty good feat for a clumsy accident-prone teen). As Bella walks 'deeper and deeper into the forest' along the damp, winding trail through 'trees' and 'ferns' (*Twilight*, p118), she is also making a choice about being with Edward and is thinking her decision through. It is there, in the 'deep green', 'high ferns', and 'piercing silence' (*Twilight*, p119) – inside the dreamy forest haze – that Bella finds her true 'answer': 'When I thought of him, of his voice, his hypnotic eyes, the magnetic force of his personality, I wanted nothing more than to be with him' (*Twilight*, p121).

Alone in a 'darkening forest' that is as 'dim as twilight under the canopy' – immersed in green and peaceful ambience – Bella makes a choice that changes her life drastically. Forever. She chooses Edward.

In fact, the deep forest scenery appears to reflect the decision-making process deep inside Bella's mind. Bella's ability to move easily through the dark forest maze matches her ability to navigate a complex psychological issue. When Bella reaches a deep, thick part of the forest (looks deep inside her mind/heart, get it?), and sits down to rest in a 'private place' where no one can 'see her' (*Twilight*, p119), that's when she chooses what she truly, 'privately desires' – Edward. In the 'dim twilight' of this forest, Bella's choice reflects a twilight time (time of change) in her own life. Shortly after this forest visit, Bella's choice to be with Edward crystallizes and her confidence becomes more established. 'My decision was made' (*Twilight*, p217), she concludes. Bella then confirms her decision: 'I'd made my choice, and I wasn't going back on it' (*Twilight*, p220).

The psychological message? To find your true place in the world, it is so important to make a choice that supports your true inner needs and desires.

How do we know that Bella's choice to be with Edward was a good one? A number of indicators suggest that Bella's choice is likely to make her truly happy.

## Happiness Involves Exploring Your Inner Self

Bella's hike in the forest is a metaphor that means Bella is exploring her innermost self. People who know, understand, and appreciate themselves better attract powerful psychological benefits. Behavior experts Dr le Roux and Dr de Klerk explain that:

> If you know yourself, you know your strengths and growth areas. You are able to accept yourself more easily and you can fulfill your potential. If you receive feedback from others, you are able to determine whether it is valid or invalid.

A choice based on honest self-knowledge leads the way to true happiness.

## Happiness Is Embracing Your Natural Coping Style

When you pressure people to make choices that are inappropriate for them, not only do things not work out, it can make people feel like failures on top of already feeling miserable. A psychology professor and the founding director of the Centre of Applied Positive Psychology in the United Kingdom is Dr Alex Linley. He defines a strength as 'a pre-existing capacity for a particular way of behaving, thinking, or feeling that is authentic and energizing to the user, and enables optimal functioning, development and performance'. In Twilight vampire terms, this means that using your 'gifts' will help you to feel truly happy and empower you to achieve your goals. Research shows that people who tap into their 'signature strengths', as happiness expert Professor Seligman calls them, report an increase in positive experiences, which includes higher levels of:

- Happiness and satisfaction

- Energy and vitality
- Personal control
- Self-esteem

In the Twilight series, for example, Jacob is delighted at the idea of putting his *mechanical* ability to use, by fixing up a couple of old motorbikes that Bella brings to his place. Interacting with Bella will also enable him to tap into his sunny *social* strengths. In fact, Jacob looked 'truly pleased by the challenge' and his 'face glowed' with happiness (*Eclipse*, p134).

## Happiness Is Living Your Values

Another indication that your choices will make you happy is if they support your personal values. If you aren't living according to your true interests and personal values, you won't be happy, no matter what you have, who you're with, or how much you achieve. Psychologist and self-esteem expert Dr Nathaniel Brandon says that: 'Happiness or joy is the emotional state that proceeds from the achievement of one's values. Suffering is the emotional state that proceeds from a negation or destruction of one's values.'

The Twilight world certainly highlights this valuable point about values. Edward tried to exist without Bella in his life, but despite traveling to Alaska and South America and Italy, he couldn't. Jacob tried to establish a romantic relationship with Bella, even though he hadn't authentically imprinted on her, but couldn't. Renee tried to live in Forks and be a good wife to a man married to his job, but couldn't. Carlisle tried to fit in with the Volturi aristocrats, but couldn't. If you deny your true calling, turn against your own beliefs, try to be something you're not, and dismiss your inner self, you might find many interesting things – but *not* true happiness.

When Bella was human, she felt depressed. In her new role as a vampire, Bella feels 'overwhelming ecstasy' and 'euphoric the vast majority of the time' (*Breaking Dawn*, p488). Why is Bella so freakin' happy? Was it the island honeymoon? The stone cottage? The clothes? The kid? Or those gorgeous crimson eyes just before feeding time? According to positive psychology, the main reason why Bella is *so* happy as a vampire is because she has always chosen this path. Her experience affirms her deepest and truest values:

> I had been born to be a vampire. The idea made me want to laugh, but it also made me want to sing. I had found my true place in the world, the place I fit, the place I shined.
> (*Breaking Dawn*, p485)

To find your true place in *your* world, you need to ask yourself this important question: '*If I just had one chance to do what I really, truly wanted to do with my life, what would that be?*' To find the best possible answer, you must explore the deep forests of your mind – and make a choice that echoes your innermost voice. Only then can you create a positive and shiny vision for the future and start hiking your way towards it.

## Jacob: Doomed to Obey?

> *We have to kill . . .*
> *We have a duty to fulfil.*
> I braced myself. *No.*
> Sam snarled and stopped pacing in front of me . . .
> *Yes,* the Alpha decreed, his double voice blistering with the heat of his authority.
> (*Breaking Dawn*, p184, p188–189)

In a werewolf world, fate is fixed, firm, forced. The scene above reveals the pack's plan to kill Bella Swan and the Cullens. The pack laws must be followed. The wolves must obey their leader.

No exceptions. Well, not until Jacob Black takes a stand and makes a choice that changes everything.

Despite Sam's tough leadership style, Jacob disobeys him. Jacob's choice significantly changes his own destiny and the destiny of others. A moral disagreement with the wolf boss drew out Jacob's confidence to think for himself, look outside the square, and look inside himself. Jacob refuses to help the pack kill innocent individuals who have never harmed him or his community. As Jacob tells the Alpha: '*I won't follow you, Sam. Not for something so wrong*' (*Breaking Dawn*, p193). A situational crisis compelled Jacob to discover his inner values and make a clear choice that confirmed those values. As a consequence, however, Jacob must leave his home, his family, his territory and his old lifestyle behind. This critical choice point opens up a whole new world for Jacob and transforms him into a social leader.

In the history of the real world to this day, people have always fought for freedom and important beliefs. The Greenpeace anti-whaling campaign and the anti-Apartheid movement in Africa are just two outstanding examples of passionate and admirable crusades. Many people would rather stand up to oppressive rule than live on their knees in fear and slavery. Rather than let destiny dictate, Jacob made his biggest choice ever. Yes, Jacob became a loner. Yes, Jacob made enemies. But he is autonomous, honest and free. It's these kinds of choices that make people successful inventors, pioneers, leaders, champions, and heroes. Why are 'perpetually happy' people like Jacob so rebellious? Maybe Abraham Maslow's theory can provide some insight.

## Maslow's Motivation Theory

According to Maslow's famous motivational theory, people have a hierarchy of needs. Once people satisfy basic needs like food, safety, shelter, and self-esteem, they strive to fulfill other higher needs. Maslow calls this upper level of metaneeds 'self-actualization'. It is a constructive process of functioning optimally to fulfill one's potential. It is characterized by acceptance, autonomy, realistic thinking, creativity, high ethics, and personal growth. In other words, the happiest, healthiest, and most self-actualized people tend to be:

- Honest – they take responsibility for what they think and feel
- Self-directed – they do not conform to views thoughtlessly, just to be popular
- Inner-directed – they listen to their inner voice, not the voice of an authority figure
- Inspired – they are willing to apply themselves to achieve their best.

This sounds a lot like Jacob to me.

While it may seem be easier to please everyone just to be popular, you cannot win. It is impossible to please everyone. If you try to do it, some people will still not like you. They will think of you as a pushover or someone who is easy to bully or manipulate. If you try to please some of the people, all the others will not agree with what you do. Charles Mackay penned a rhyme that describes this psychological dilemma in a work called 'No Enemies':

*You have no enemies, you say?*
*Alas, my friend, the boast is poor.*
*He who has mingled in the fray*
*Of duty, that the brave endure,*
*Must have made foes. If you have none,*
*Small is the work that you have done.*
*You've hit no traitor on the hip,*
*You've dashed no cup from perjured lip,*
*You've never turned the wrong to right,*
*You've been a coward in the fight.*

As this verse suggests, Jacob has chosen a path that others hate and this has created enemies among wolves. Psychologically, however, Jacob is probably less likely to feel guilty and suffer in the long term because his choice does not conflict with his inner values. Had Jacob tried to please the pack and not offend Sam, that response would have been cowardly, a devaluation of himself and his beliefs. If you try to obey everyone all the time, you are doomed to fail.

As a matter of fact, it may be helpful to keep in mind that an excessive tendency to please others produces considerable anxiety and can lead to severe anxiety disorders. As *The Anxiety and Phobia Workbook* explains, that is why so many anxiety sufferers benefit from assertiveness skills training. This helps under-assertive people recognize their basic rights and stick up for themselves.

To experience genuine happiness, increase control over your life, and find your true place in the world, it is crucial to discover the true you. Your faith in yourself and your beliefs will make your happiness stronger for longer, making it much harder for others to find cracks and weak spots in your choices.

## Increase Authentic Happiness

Can people like Bella experience happiness in a lasting and fulfilling way? Are there any excellent psychological adventures from the Twilight books worth noting? Certainly, positive psychology research shows that when people receive happiness-increasing information and apply positive strategies to improve their thinking and behavior, they can make lasting improvements to their happiness. After drawing together all the existing knowledge and research evidence on happiness to date, authentic happiness expert Professor Martin Seligman outlined the most effective ways to increase happiness:

1 Get more pleasure out of life.

2 Become more engaged in what you do, and
3 Find ways to make your life feel more meaningful.

To achieve authentic happiness (ongoing and fulfilling happiness), it is important to work on all three parts.

## The Pleasures of Life

> 'The back wall had big glass doors that opened into a little hidden garden. Climbing roses and a small round pond, smooth as a mirror and edged with shiny stones' (*Breaking Dawn*, p445).

In the Twilight world, the rose garden outside Bella and Edward's cottage is a little pleasure paradise. The beauty and magic of the garden make it a good example of something that can be used to increase happiness. Just reading about the rose garden starts to stimulate senses such as sight ('climbing roses') and smell (the perfume of 'roses').

According to positive psychology, the quickest and easiest way to increase happiness is to experience pleasure, perhaps by visiting a little rose garden like the one above. Not only are pleasure-promoting activities suitable for people who just want to boost their happiness levels; they also provide an excellent way to help really depressed or anxious people who might find it hard to motivate themselves to go out and do things. That is why psychologists like Dr George Burns have developed fun and simple happiness strategies for really depressed people. An easy and simple 'pleasure program' can involve tasks such as:

1 Participating in pleasurable activities
2 Acknowledging the good things in life, and
3 Doing simple activities that please the senses (sight, sound, touch, taste, smell).

These strategies can be used to increase anyone's feelings of happiness or decrease feelings of depression.

Imagine that Bella was feeling really depressed, didn't feel up to doing much, and we wanted to improve her happiness and health. We could apply some positive psychology strategies to enhance her feelings of pleasure:

### Bella's Pleasure Plan

- Do a pleasurable activity every day
- Visit a bookshop in Port Angeles
- Go on a motorbike ride with Jacob (as passenger, with helmet)
- Watch a comedy movie with Dad

### Acknowledge good things

To further increase pleasure and develop a positive attitude, Bella could write down three things she is grateful for every day. For example, Bella's list of ideas might include:

1. 'I'm grateful that I graduated high school.'
2. 'My parents care about me.'
3. 'Meeting the Cullens and the Quileutes makes my life interesting.'

### Experience sensory pleasure

People who study long hours, work very hard, or shut themselves up in a room all day for weeks because they feel really depressed or anxious are suffering badly from sensory deprivation. To make the senses feel alive again, people such as Bella could do little things every day (even if it's just five minutes long to begin with) to stimulate the five basic senses. For example, Bella could create a list of things that please her senses and experience three things from that list each day:

## Things that May Please Bella's Senses

| Sight | Sound | Smell | Taste | Touch | Favourite Activity |
|---|---|---|---|---|---|
| Watch sunlight sparkling on snow in Forks<br><br>Look into Edward's liquid–topaz eyes | Hear forest birds singing<br><br>Listen to Edward playing the piano | Inhale the perfume of roses and other flowers<br><br>Notice the sweet smell of forest pine trees | Taste wild forest fruits in summer<br><br>Eat mushroom ravioli | Feel the cool forest shade in summer<br><br>Hug Jacob (as a warm human or a furry wolf) | Sunset picnic at La Push beach |

(Based on the Sensory Awareness Inventory designed by Dr Burns)

To experience sensory pleasure as fully and deeply as possible, Bella could go multimodal. That is, she could try to treat three different sense modes each day. For example, Bella could get maximum pleasure from her rosebushes by:

- Looking at the roses in the cottage garden (sight)
- Inhaling the beautiful fragrance of the roses (smell)
- Scattering silky-soft rose petals onto her bed (touch)
- Creating sugar-coated rose petal sweets (taste)

These simple happiness-increasing activities help people to 1) increase their awareness of pleasure, 2) immerse themselves in sensory pleasure, 3) appreciate and absorb the moment more fully, and 4) savor positive experiences.

### Engage with Life

The Twilight world also shows that another way to increase authentic happiness is to be actively engaged with life. This means being actively involved in enjoyable and stimulating activities that involve some attention or skill.

### Edward's Music

An elegant example of *engagement* from the Twilight series is when Edward plays the piano for Bella:

> His fingers flowed swiftly across the ivory, and the room was filled with a composition so complex, so luxuriant, it was impossible to believe only one set of hands played . . .
>
> 'Do you like it?'
>
> 'You wrote this?' I gasped, understanding.
>
> (*Twilight*, p285)

Edward doesn't simply hit black and white keys in the right sequence. He is fully absorbed and engaged in his task. Edward and Bella seem to lose themselves in the music, forgetting about their worries and woes for a while. Edward might be a 'glorious angel' (*Twilight*, p212) to Bella. But as this scene suggests, Bella is definitely Edward's divine Muse. Visited by a Muse, a spirit of inspiration from Greek myth, Edward composed this music for Bella. 'You inspired this one' (*Twilight*, p285), Edward tells her.

According to positive psychology, when people become engaged, involved, and absorbed in interesting activities (in the areas of work, leisure, or relationships), they experience increased authentic happiness. Professor Seligman says that:

> . . . one might be engaged in a good book, focused on a talk at work, absorbed in a movie, intimately engaged in making love, or involved in helping one another. One way to build the engaged life is to help a person identify his or her highest strengths, skills, or resources and then to engage in using those strengths more.

For example, Edward uses his well-developed musical ability to hum a lullaby for Bella, to help her sleep (*Twilight*, p272). Edward also used his musical talents to record a CD for Bella's birthday (*New Moon*, p49). These engaging activities enhance Edward's experience of authentic happiness.

Another important example of musical engagement from a different Twilight Saga character is when Bella's mother performed music: 'I loved to watch her play. She was happy, absorbed – she seemed like a new, mysterious being to me then, someone outside the "mom" persona I took for granted' (*Twilight*, p284).

When Bella recalls watching her mother play the piano, she also recalls the passion, purpose, and power that her mother expressed when engaged in an enjoyable activity. Maybe Bella's mother developed the supposed 'flighty personality' critics claim she has because, for whatever reason, she was compelled to disengage from her favorite activities – activities like music, travel, adventure, which would have utilized her 'signature strengths' such as 'creativity'.

A few other brief examples of strength-based engagement from the Twilight books:

- Bella can 'cook' and she prepares healthy and tasty meals for her father, which he really appreciates.
- Jacob uses his 'woodwork design' skills to craft a beautiful gift for Bella.
- Alice's 'artistic' streak helps her to plan and prepare the liveliest and most colorful parties around Forks.

The trick to authentic happiness is investing time and energy in activities that show off your personal strengths. Not only do various adventures from the Twilight books increase insight into the experiences of our favorite characters, you can use your newly found insights to think about *your* special strengths and how you might use them in your life. Are you a natural-born leader, thinker, inventor, or writer? Do you love sport? Are you good with animals? Are you a 'perpetually funny' clown? Those who identify and engage their psychological strengths in work, play, or relationships, will increase their experience of authentic happiness, for sure.

### A Meaningful Life

In the area of positive psychology, living a meaningful life is a leading happiness factor. When people have a meaningful purpose, direction, or goal in life, they feel happier, healthier, and much more satisfied with the quality of life. A number of important Twilight characters help to show that doing meaningful things increases authentic happiness. Of course, the opposite of happiness is depression, which involves the absence of meaning in life.

In the world of Twilight, the lives of many favorite characters change positively and dramatically once they find personal meaning in life:

- Bella declares to Edward 'You are the most important thing to me now' (*Twilight*, p240). Her life feels 'right' and has meaning with Edward in it (*New Moon*, p69).
- Edward's life is much more meaningful after he falls in love with Bella. It makes him be more 'optimistic' and 'laugh more' (*Twilight*, p264). Esme confirms that Bella is 'what he wants' (*Twilight*, p322).
- A content and proud moment for Jacob is when he listens to Quileute legends about his spiritual ancestry (*Eclipse*, p230).
- Jasper was very 'depressed' and 'wandered on his own' until Alice found him and gave him a positive reason to live (*Twilight*, p258).
- Rosalie's life was filled with painful memories of her

fiancé's brutal attack until she saved her strong and sweet Emmett from a grizzly bear (*Twilight*, p252).

## Carlisle's Meaningful Medicine

With regards to the positive effects of living a meaningful life, one of the most instructive characters in the Twilight world is Dr Carlisle Cullen. When Carlisle was first turned into a vampire, he was unhappy, lonely, and afraid. Murdering people in order to drink their blood meant the worst and most monstrous things to him, and he felt condemned to a miserable eternal afterlife. A life that had no positive meaning for him. At first, Carlisle tried to cope with his new existence in various ways:

- Attempting suicide (jumping from great heights, drowning)
- Starving himself
- Exiling himself from the human population
- Trying to come to terms with what he had become: a vampire

(*Twilight*, p294–295)

After much suffering, Carlisle accidentally discovered that he could survive on animal blood and did not have to feed on humans. For Carlisle, this meant a great deal because 'he could exist without being a demon' (*Twilight*, p295). This gave Carlisle hope and he began to use his time more productively. As Edward explains: 'Carlisle swam to France, and continued on through Europe, to the universities there. By night, he studied music, science, medicine – and found his calling, his penance, in that, in saving human lives' (*Twilight*, p297).

Highly 'intelligent' and 'compassionate' by nature, Carlisle evolved in a way that enabled him to use his 'signature strengths' and pursue things that meant a lot to him. He studied and became a doctor, healing others and saving lives. By expressing his true inner nature – his compassion and intelligence – Carlisle eventually found positive meaning in life. This dramatically increased his feelings of personal contentment, life satisfaction, and authentic happiness.

In *New Moon*, Carlisle confirms the importance of positive psychology's 'meaningfulness' factor. Unhappy as a vampire, Carlisle figured out a positive and meaningful way to use his new abilities and heightened senses without harming humans. The medical studies have paid off because Carlisle enjoys being a doctor so much. As Carlisle explains to Bella: '"What I enjoy the very most is when my . . . enhanced abilities let me save someone who would otherwise have been lost. It's pleasant knowing that, thanks to what I can do, some people's lives are better because I exist' (*New Moon*, p34).

As the case of Carlisle suggests, when people use their natural strengths in positive ways that align with their values, this strategy increases meaning and produces authentic feelings of happiness.

Some strategies that Twilight characters use to find meaning and increase authentic happiness are consistent with those recommended by positive psychologists. For example:

### Thank someone

Thanking someone to whom you owe a debt of gratitude, such as a friend, teacher, or relative, helps people to develop positive appraisal skills and encourages people to acknowledge positive things in life. Studies show that people who write a thank-you letter to someone (and then read the letter to that person) are continually and measurably happier for more than a month. Edward, for example, likes to use this strategy. In one of his letters, Edward writes: 'Jacob . . . Thank you – for her – for everything. Edward' (*Eclipse*, p557).

### Perform kind actions

Positive psychology research shows that when people perform five small acts of kindness for a week, this creates a noticeable increase to happiness levels. Giving not only makes you feel good about yourself; it also enhances your connection with others and attracts positive feedback from others. In the Twilight world, for example, Alice's sad childhood involved being deserted by her parents, who left her at an asylum as a baby. Nevertheless, Alice gains enormous pleasure and meaning in life by being 'perpetually kind' to others and making other people's lives happier. She uses her artistic flair (her signature strength) to pick out fancy clothes for Bella (*Twilight*, p420), plan birthday parties (*New Moon*, p10), and organize high school celebrations (*Eclipse*, 325). Alice loves Jasper deeply, and offers him a highly 'supportive' and affectionate 'climate' that he needs, enjoys, and thrives in (*Eclipse*, 268).

### Connect to a larger purpose

Philosophical, spiritual, or religious activities provide a significant source of meaning for most people. A life that is guided by a higher purpose such as 'increasing knowledge' (e.g. finishing school, studying a trade, attending university) or supporting a 'greater cause' (e.g. charity work, cancer research, caring for the environment, saving whales and dolphins) boosts authentic happiness. In the Twilight Saga, Carlisle and Esme enjoy fostering and looking after teen vampires. It gives them meaning and satisfaction to help others in need. That is why Carlisle offered to care for the newborn teenage vampire Bree (*Eclipse*, p512).

A number of important characters in the Twilight books help to show that authentic happiness can be increased and maintained by enhancing pleasure, engagement, and meaning. If you are feeling depressed or anxious, you can begin to increase your happiness by enjoying simple and immediate pleasures.

Later on, you can explore and experiment with more engaging and meaningful activities. A powerful psychological message hidden in the Twilight Saga is that if you want to be really happy, what you need is to create a positive psychological adventure.

## The Happiness Game

### Choice

> 'I've never seen anyone go through this who's chosen it beforehand' (*Eclipse*, p516).

In the Twilight world, Bella *chooses* to become a vampire. This makes the two chess pieces (red pawn, white queen) on the original *Breaking Dawn* book cover meaningful psychological symbols. You see, they help to show that the quest for authentic happiness is strategic, not fate-driven, much like playing a game of chess. Despite the playing field before you and the pieces life deals you, it's the positive choices and smart sequence of moves in a game that matter.

Bella's quest to be happy starts off with a somewhat strained childhood. In *Twilight*, for example, Bella is a shy and lonely girl who describes an emotionally distant father and a carefree mother. Her old clothes, untidy hair, and clumsy behavior set her at a lower standard to her peers and make her a social misfit. However, the experience of needing to look after herself as well as her parents develops Bella's emotional maturity and helps her to become a more autonomous and spirited individual. A shunned and ignored only child, this compels Bella to search for deeper meanings in life.

Then Bella moves to Forks and meets Edward at her new school. Her uncanny intuition enables her to pick up super-natural forces at work around her and she strongly senses that Edward is a good person. Bella decides to get to know him better and concludes that Edward is her true love in life. In order to fulfill her quest and achieve authentic happiness, Bella makes a series of positive, productive, and profitable choices. For example, Bella chooses to search for knowledge, sacrifices herself to save others, and adapts to her human and supernatural worlds at Forks open-mindedly.

## Change

Bella's quest for happiness involves great psychological change. By opening her heart and mind, she starts to move through life in ways she never did before – deep inside forests, fast in Edward's car, at super-speed on Edward's back, in underground vampire tunnels, and through time when listening to Cullen family history and ancient Quileute legends. As Bella descends into dark forest places, deep under water, and into the mysterious world of dreams, she is also descending deep into her unconscious mind. It's only after Bella confronts a human hunter alone in a ballet studio (a place that trains people to move gracefully) that is full of mirrors (mirrors symbolize deep reflection of the inner self), that Bella finally confronts herself honestly and makes her most important choice of all. She asks Edward to turn her into a vampire (*Twilight*, p411).

As a result of her choices, Bella is no longer a 'pawn' whose life is controlled by fate and outside influences such as her parents' separation, the gloomy Forks weather, and the threat of evil vampires. Bella transforms herself into a confident young woman who is in control of her life – a powerful queen who uses her signature strengths like her empathy 'shield' to conquer a life-size battlefield. With her cleverness, courage, and a strong desire to protect loved ones, Bella defies the dangerous Volturi vampires.

## Checkmate

As positive psychology theory predicts and Bella Swan shows, choice determines authentic happiness. Bella fulfilled her quest and wins the biggest game ever, *not* because she is:

- Physically powerful – characters like Jacob or Emmett are far more athletic and stronger than Bella.
- Highly educated – Bella has only just finished high school. She does not have a medical degree like Dr Cullen nor centuries of intellectual learning like the Volturi.
- Wealthy – Bella does not come from a high income family.
- Experienced – Bella is a teenager who has not yet had decades of life experience.

Rather, Bella found true happiness because she chose to. As such, Bella delivers an important psychological message. The strongest, smartest, richest, most experienced, or most educated individuals do not necessarily find happiness, conquer destiny, and achieve success. *The one who succeeds is the one who makes the best possible choices in life.*

Choices produce champions. They can take you to amazing places that you never thought possible. Bella's series of choices and her decision to become a vampire helped Bella to fulfill her personal quest and find true happiness – *checkmate!*

# 7

# I Sparkle: Experience a Spiritual Saga

*People are like stained-glass windows. They sparkle and shine when the sun is out, but when the darkness sets in, their true beauty is revealed only if there is a light from within.*
- Elisabeth Kubler-Ross, psychiatrist

## Twilight Sparkles Spiritually

How can a story about a bunch of teenagers, a pack of werewolves, and soulless vampires be *spiritual*? Actually, underneath the romance, danger, sharp fangs and bloody battles, the Twilight books should definitely be rated 'S' due to strong 'spiritual' themes. A really important message that the novels deliver is that no matter how bad things are in life, you can advance yourself in this life – and the next. The prominent 19th-century writer Oscar Wilde once wrote: 'We are all in the gutter, but some of us are looking at the stars.' As Bella, Edward, Jacob and the Cullens show, spiritual well-being involves discovering a higher purpose and trying to reach the stars. This may involve loving others, helping others, connecting to the universe, or undergoing a deep personal change. The best stories ever written are those that inspire us, stimulate us, change us, and take us somewhere happier, somewhere higher, somewhere better. And the Twilight Saga is such a story – shooting across the sky like a comet, with brilliant ideas that have the power to stir you long after you have finished reading the books. The Twilight world sparkles spiritually in a way that both entertains and empowers.

## Transpersonal Psychology Rises

## What is Transpersonal Psychology?

As a deeply spiritual tale, the Twilight Saga alludes to the field of transpersonal psychology – an area that concerns the spiritual aspects of human experience. The *Journal of Transpersonal Psychology,* first published in 1969, says that transpersonal psychology 'is concerned with the study of humanity's highest potential, and with the recognition, understanding, and realization of unitive, spiritual, and transcendent states of consciousness' (Lajoie and Shapiro, 1992). The themes of transpersonal psychology include advanced states of consciousness, a sense of higher purpose, acting for the greater good, self-transcendence, and spiritual life. Even The National Aboriginal Community Controlled Organisation defines mental health as 'not just the physical well-being of the individual, but the social, emotional, spiritual and cultural well-being of the whole community. This is a whole of life view and it includes the concept of life-death-life'.

Transpersonal psychology, a spin-off of humanistic psychology, has been considered the most complete and integrated positive psychology to date because it acknowledges the *soul,* which previous psychology theories do not. A significant benefit of this approach is that it supports people suffering serious illness, death, disasters, and other significant life crises. Other rich rewards of this 'fourth wave' of psychology include giving people good ideas and strategies to promote positive thinking, healing, salvation, or enlightenment. These spiritual aspects facilitate a more meaningful and satisfying life.

## The Search for Meaning

To sparkle spiritually, you must first get a twinkle in your eye – find your passion, identify your dream, notice the stars, uncover a purpose. As Bella's inner mind once suggested in a dream, the only way to fulfill life is to find meaning: 'I hurried through the gloom without a path, always searching, searching, searching' (*New Moon*, p123).

The famous psychiatrist Dr Viktor Frankl is a leading existential analyst (*existential* means 'relating to existence'). He developed a transpersonal approach called *logotherapy* (the Greek word *logos* means 'word', 'spirit', or 'meaning'). Dr Frankl believes that people are basically looking for meaning and purpose in life. Since people desire to pursue some great and worthy goal, people need freedom of expression and personal responsibility to create a purposeful life. Above all, Dr Frankl says that:

- Meaning must be found and cannot be given.
- Meaning is something to discover rather than to invent.

This suggests that every person must search for meaning themselves – the same idea captured in Bella's dream.

When people eventually integrate and make sense of all the information in their world, discovering a point to it all, life feels meaningful and people are on a path to progress. People who discover a purpose in life and connect to forces far greater than themselves (like the universe, eternity, and spiritual values) are much happier, healthier, and satisfied with life. In line with existential psychology, our favorite Twilight characters are using effective transpersonal tricks to give themselves a spiritual edge.

## Twilight Takes Life Higher

As the world of Twilight shows and a branch called transpersonal psychology explains, people can find meaning in life and grow spiritually in a number of ways. One way is to experience something really special, significant and powerful. Another approach is to take action that supports the greater good. Other ways include keeping an open mind about the existence of higher forces. As you will see, different Twilight characters use different approaches to advance themselves transpersonally and take their lives higher.

## Bella's Higher Experience

An important way to find higher purpose in life and develop spiritual power is through *personal experience*. This involves experiencing something or someone meaningful – with regards to free time, work, or love. A higher experience can include:

- A mind-blowing experience such as viewing great art, attending an opera, visiting natural wonders, or watching someone commit a heroic act
- A mind-broadening experience such as traveling overseas, helping poor folk, sailing solo around the world
- The experience of love

The love Bella feels for Edward, and others, is her higher experience because it gives her so much meaning and direction in life. In transpersonal psychology, love is supposed to derive from the spiritual unconscious, that is, the higher conscience. Love, says Dr Frankl, 'is the ultimate and the highest goal to which people can aspire'.

In many adventures, Bella shows that her higher experience is love because she is willing to sacrifice her human life to be with a vampire. She also shows higher love because she repeatedly sacrifices her own life to save those she loves. Examples of Bella's love-driven experiential purpose in life:

- Bella leaves Arizona so that her mum can be happy with her new partner (*Twilight*, p42).
- Bella tells Edward: 'I would rather die than stay away from you' (*Twilight*, p240).
- During an intimate embrace, Bella loves Edward so much that she, knowing he is a dangerous predator and can kill

her, risks her life to be in love with him: 'I knew any moment it could be too much, and my life could end' (*Twilight*, p242).

- She leads an evil vampire away from her father's house to protect him (*Twilight*, p343).
- She sacrifices her own life to save her mother (*Twilight*, p374).
- She does not alert Edward or his family that she plans to meet a murderous vampire at the ballet studio, as she does not want to risk the lives of those she loves (*Twilight*, p392).
- She travels to Volterra in Italy to save Edward from suicide (*New Moon*).
- She is willing to die in Edward's place; she tells the Volturi, 'kill me' (*New Moon*).
- She cuts her arm to distract Victoria from attacking Edward (*Eclipse*).

A deep and meaningful experience of love enables Bella to evolve spiritually and move towards soulish enlightenment. What's more, the Twilight world shows that love can be a very important spiritual experience, just as transpersonal psychology suggests. In particular:

- Edward suggests that Bella is his 'soul-mate' when he tells her 'you've taken half myself away with you' (*Twilight*, p365).
- Jacob explains that 'imprinting' is how werewolves fall in love and find their 'soul-mates' (*Eclipse*, p109).
- Alice is always 'watching out for Jasper's future. He was her soul mate, her true other half' (*Eclipse*, p44).

These higher experiences involving love suggest that the Twilight characters feel a love that is deep and transpersonal in nature. Experiencing something – or someone – we truly value gives people great meaning and invigorates the soul. For Bella, Edward, Jacob, and other caring characters, love is a slice of heaven. It is a step higher on the staircase to some sort of experiential paradise, one move closer to the upper spiritual plane.

When Dr Frankl was a World War Two prisoner in a Nazi concentration camp, and he did not know if his wife was alive or not, he decided that it really did not matter after all. This is because:

> I knew only one thing . . . nothing could touch the strength of my love, my thoughts, and the image of my beloved.
>
> Love goes very far beyond the physical person of the beloved. It finds its deepest meaning in his spiritual being, his inner self. Whether or not he is actually present, whether or not he is still alive at all, ceases somehow to be of importance.
>
> There was no need for me to know.

To survive the depressing and desolate atmosphere of the prison camps, Dr Frankl would often talk to his wife – even though she wasn't there. 'The guard passed by, insulting me, and once again I communed with my beloved,' he says. Is this the behavior of a nutty professor? No, it is a bright spiritual sparkle – a crucial transpersonal survival tip. No matter what happens, a person is free to view reality in a much higher and more meaningful way. The transpersonal point here is that love is an untouchable, unbeatable, and invisible force that does not just exist in the physical and mortal world. There is a higher spiritual love that persists and prospers too. An everlasting kind of love that Bella and Edward will always have for each other, regardless of whether they are human or vampire, mortal or supernatural, dead or alive.

As the former First Lady of the United States Eleanor Roosevelt explains and Bella's higher love for Edward illustrates: 'The purpose of life, after all, is to live it, to taste the experience to the utmost, to reach out eagerly and without fear for newer and richer experience.'

## The Cullens' Higher Actions

Another way to discover meaning in life and promote spiritual growth is by taking higher action. An individual can express positive and creative values by 'doing good deeds'. This is one of the first and most important things that Bella learns about the Cullens: '*Stregoni benefici: An Italian vampire, said to be on the side of goodness*' (*Twilight*, p117).

A traditional existential way to take life higher is to become involved in meaningful projects. This taps into the power of creativity, which can be used in art, music, writing, invention, business, science and so on. Frankl views 'creativity' as a function of the spiritual unconscious. It is a passionate, irrational and fiery ability that higher forces inspire. Acting for the greater good – performing higher actions – is a path to spiritual enlightenment.

As far as the Cullens are concerned, they achieve a sense of purpose in life creatively – through their 'eco-friendly' deeds, for example. The Cullen vampires develop themselves transpersonally by considering other people, their environment, and adopting a 'vegetarian' lifestyle. By considering nature and not killing humans, the Cullens do not express harmful actions and negative energy. These positive behaviors would promote feelings of peace, oneness, wholeness with nature and the universe – spiritual growth and psychological well-being.

One of the best examples showing off the Cullens' commitment to higher actions is when Edward explains their new-age food-gathering practices to Bella. Not only do the Cullens refrain from drinking the blood of humans, they also use ethical procedures when hunting animals: 'We have to be careful not to impact the environment with injudicious hunting. We try to focus on areas with an overpopulation of predators – ranging as far away as we need. There's always plenty of deer and elk here' (*Twilight*, p188).

The Cullens live a vegetarian lifestyle and care about their impact on the natural environment. They have replaced greedy and self-centered behavior with higher actions, for example: vegetarian eating habits, not killing humans, feeding only to survive, helping the environment, stopping unnecessary suffering of animals, helping to protect endangered animal species, and only culling animal population explosions to restore environmental balance. In all, the Cullens have evolved psychologically, morally, spiritually because they express positive and creative deeds to support a higher purpose.

Since the Cullens' nature-friendly deeds are an attempt to live harmoniously with the rest of the environment, rather than control or exploit nature, their actions fit with other important definitions of spirituality. A scientific health journal defines spirituality as 'the inner essence of a person . . . a sense of harmonious interconnectedness with self, others, nature and an ultimate other'. The Cullens' approach supports this view, in that they respect all things in nature. Some of the wisest cultures in the world relate to nature in the same higher way.

Did you know that according to Quileute legend, the land around Forks was once the battleground of giant supernatural monsters? A Quileute creation myth explains that the mountains, valleys, boulders, rivers were formed by great spiritual beings who fought each other long ago. As neither creature could win the battle, they withdrew to the caves and cried steaming hot tears. Their fighting ground formed the hot springs of the Forks region that you can visit today (www.quileutenation.org, March 30, 2011). These spiritual stories help the Quileute people care for nature to this day.

In East Europe, where vampire legends originally come from, people also saw nature as being spiritually alive. They saw rugged and beautiful natural habitats as being inhabited by fabulous creatures who protected forests, meadows, mountains, rivers and lakes to maintain order in their wild abodes. This spiritual and non-human-centered view of the world encouraged people to relate more closely to nature, respect nature, and show ecological care (www.arts.ualberta.ca, March 29, 2011).

These days, most people live in big cities, like the Volturi do, never venturing out into the countryside. With so much of the natural world being destroyed, many people are losing their connections with the magical and spiritual side of nature. Their higher actions are diminishing. Spiritual expert Sirona Knight observes that people in the modern world have 'little or no time to enjoy recreation outdoors in forests or meadows or by lakes, rivers or the ocean. This lack of outdoor recreation leads to more alienation and separation from the Earth. In turn, we become more distant and apart from ourselves and our spiritual center'.

The nature-friendly Cullens present a powerful spiritual message. We can all protect beautiful forests and wild seashores like those at La Push and reconnect with nature. Everyone can perform higher ecological actions to restore and reclaim the great green spirit. Recently, the Quileutes celebrated nature. The Quileute Tribal Council hosted an event to welcome migrating gray whales, referring to these magnificent creatures are 'our kin . . . We will now begin the day with events that uplift our spiritual relationship with the grays, orcas, and other whales as they return, live, and swim to bless our waters and enhance us with good fortune'. In transpersonal psychology, it matters what we do. Productively or destructively, creatively or wastefully, through low-life deeds or higher efforts, our actions determine the quality of our psychological and spiritual life.

## Carlisle's Highest Wish

## Supra-Meaning

Is there a soul?

Can individuals lose their souls?

What kind of power determines the existence of everything and everyone in the first place?

This timeless philosophical discussion thread has finally been joined by some new blood – Twilight vampires and psychologists. The Twilight character who seems to have contemplated these spiritual issues the most is Dr Carlisle Cullen. He has wandered alone for years, suffered, fasted, experimented, meditated, traveled abroad, lived with the Volturi vampires in Italy, and has studied art and science in an attempt to find adequate answers to these deep existential questions. Above all, Carlisle has searched for the highest possible meaning in life, which existential psychologists call *supra-meaning*. In the Twilight books, Bella's search for higher meaning has been *experiential* (e.g. finding love) and the Cullens' search for higher meaning has been expressed through *creative actions* (e.g. eco-friendly behavior). But such meaningful behavior is only a surface manifestation of a much higher transcendence that Carlisle aspires to: *supra-*meaning. According to Dr Frankl's theory of transpersonal psychology, supra-meaning is the idea that there is an ultimate meaning to life. A meaning that does not depend on love, other people, personal actions or benevolent projects. Supra-meaning simply considers the possible existence of a supreme spiritual force.

Carlisle, for example, loves using his time to heal and save others. This enables him to have higher experiences (e.g. he enjoys being a doctor) and perform higher actions (e.g. he uses his medical skills to help others). As Carlisle describes it, he 'enjoys' saving others 'who would otherwise have been lost' and making people's lives 'better' because of his skills and existence (*New Moon*, p34). On top of this, Carlisle's spiritual development has transcended these levels of experience and action. Carlisle also understands that the mind is too limited to know everything. The mind is unable to imagine every possibility, fathom all mystical meanings, and understand how the highest powers of the universe work. As such, Carlisle has thought a lot about supra-meaning – does something exist to have made everything exist?

What if there is no spiritual realm? No paradise? No heaven? Especially if you are a goodie-goodie vampire. What's the point of Carlisle's super-compassion and productive medical actions if he is just a soulless monster? This is where Carlisle's transpersonal psychological view makes him sparkle. You see, to Carlisle, it doesn't matter: 'I'm hoping that there is still a point to this life, even for us . . . By all accounts, we're damned regardless. But I hope, maybe foolishly, that we'll get some measure of credit for trying' (*New Moon*, p36–37).

Carlisle tries to be the best vampire he can possibly be because he hopes and believes that a higher force really does exist – this is Carlisle's highest wish. An original source or a divine force might be pretty hard to prove scientifically, but the possible existence of higher spiritual power cannot be ruled out either. As such, the search to do and be better is always worth a try, even for skeptics. Carlisle's search for supra-meaning heightens his happiness, elevates his spiritual well-being, and explains why he has 'no equal' in history (*Twilight*, p252). It is meaningful to have meaning.

## Vampire Alchemy

It could be a crazy coincidence but Carlisle's super-high way of life shows in the color of his eyes and this links him to alchemy. In fact, all the Cullens have beautiful 'gold eyes'. How many times has Bella noticed the 'deep, golden honey color' of Edward's eyes (*Twilight*, p70) like 'golden butterscotch' (*Twilight*, p148) 'blazing', 'burning' and 'piercing' her with their power? (Twilight, p49, p93, p183). Other vampires also identify the Cullen clan by their 'strange yellow eyes' (*Eclipse*, p509).

Sure enough, turning lead into 'gold' is what alchemists have been trying to do all these centuries. This gold, however, is not metal or material gold. The real work of alchemy (a mix of science and mysticism) involves turning leaden human experiences into the spiritual gold of insight and enlightenment (Bennett-Goleman, 2001). In alchemy, gold symbolizes the highest possible spiritual experience and there is even a yellowing phase in alchemy known as *citrinitas* or xanthosis (en.wikipedia.org/wiki/Alchemy, May 1, 2011). Indeed, psychologists such as Carl Jung reexamined alchemy and concluded that the inner meaning of alchemical work is spiritual growth. Since Carlisle and all the Cullens have spiritual strivings and soul-searching background stories, their golden vampire eyes parallel the goldening process of spiritual alchemy.

Indeed, the Twilight world appears to have two types of vampires that can be grouped according to alchemy. As 'marrianna marinda's' 2011 insightful post points out, these 'two distinct vampire types' can be 'identified by their red eyes (human-drinking) or golden eyes (animal-drinking)' lifestyles. The mature golden-eyed Cullen vampires drink animal-blood. They also value love, peace, happiness/bliss, and gnostic/spiritual power. This contrasts the primitive crimson-eyed vampires who drink human-blood – and pursue only lust, brutality, carnal/fleshly pleasures, and material/social power. Vampires with crimson eyes have not yet evolved in a higher transpersonal way like the golden-eyed group. Rather, the vampires with dark-red eyes have deliberately prolonged a dark and bloody lifestyle for centuries that includes a diet of human blood and a brutal attitude. This has blocked them from achieving alchemy's glittering inner gold. Surely, Dr Cullen is the Twilight world's leading alchemist. This doctor-alchemist character has always sought the true gold of psychological fulfillment and sparkling spiritual brilliance for himself and others.

## Soulless

What happens when life has no meaning? No higher purpose? No spiritual direction or life? What happens when you lose your way? If adventures in the Twilight Saga are anything to by, the psychological consequences can be damaging and devastating, even deadly. The experiences of Bella and Edward certainly capture the despair that appears when reasons to live disappear. And yet, some of the best transpersonal views have emerged in the most soulless conditions in history. In particular, Dr Frank's existential views grew out of his experiences in Nazi death camps. Watching who did and did not survive (given an opportunity to survive), he observed that people who had hopes of being reunited with loved ones, or who had projects they felt a need to complete, or who had great faith, were much more likely to survive than those who had lost all hope. As long as people had a reason to live, they did live. Bella and Edward perfectly illustrate the survival value of spiritual health.

## Bella's Empty Inner Self

> 'I had died. Because it had been more than just losing the truest of true loves . . . it was also losing a whole future, a whole family – the whole life that I'd chosen' (*New Moon*, p398).

After Edward breaks up with Bella in *New Moon*, she loses her meaning in life and no longer feels alive inside. She experiences a psychological /spiritual death, not a physical death – a deep sense of loss and despair. The strongest experience that Bella reports is the 'empty feeling' inside, as if a hole was punched through her chest. For example, Bella feels like 'an empty shell. Like a vacant house. Condemned' (*New Moon*, p216). 'It was like my heart was gone – like I was hollow,' she says (*New Moon*, p515).

As well as feeling empty on the inside, the world around Bella looks empty and meaningless too, everywhere she looks:

> The meadow was empty of atmosphere, empty of everything, just like everywhere else . . . There was no way I could have disguised the abyss I was plunging into now . . . I had to curl into a ball to keep the empty space from tearing me apart.
> (*New Moon*, p234–235)

In fact, John Granger's literary analysis of the Twilight Saga reports that Bella's 'empty chest' feeling was mentioned '37 times' *in New Moon*. Dr Frankl would call this 'empty' feeling or the 'hole' in Bella's chest the *existential vacuum* – one of his favorite metaphors.

When people like Bella lose their sense of purpose in life, they then develop a profound sense of emptiness or loneliness. According to the humanistic-existential theory of psychologist Abraham Maslow, for example: 'When a person does not function according to growth motivation and the various self-actualization needs (truth, beauty, justice, and others), then he or she suffers from various kinds of spiritual disorders such as cynicism, nihilism, or emptiness.'

Poor Bella. The deep emptiness she feels is what other mental health experts sometimes call *spiritual neurosis*.

### Edward's Spiritual Crisis

Twilight Saga humans are not the only ones suffering psychologically because of spiritual reasons. Edward the vampire thinks he has no soul. As he explains to Bella: 'I know that *you* believe I have a soul, but I'm not entirely convinced' (*Eclipse*, p242). As a vampire (who drank the blood of murderers for a while) Edward insists that he is a soulless monster damned for all eternity. According to transpersonal psychology, Edward is experiencing a *spiritual crisis*. That is, a crisis that involves existential issues (issues about one's existence that transcend everyday life). Terms like 'spiritual emergence' and 'spiritual emergency', coined by Stanislav and Christina Grof in 1989, also refer to such spiritual crises in people's lives, like the one Edward is having. Spiritual crises can be stirred up by mystical experiences, near-death experiences, meditation, or even terminal illnesses like cancer. Edward's view that vampires have no soul worries him a lot.

Since Edward's spiritual crisis is the belief that vampires have no souls, he does not wish to turn Bella into a vampire because he does not want to destroy her human soul. Edward's father Carlisle explains: 'You see, he thinks we've lost our souls' (*New Moon*, p37). Edward's spiritual view is so strong that it has drastically affected his psychological well-being his relationships with others, and it nearly cost him his life. In *New Moon*, Edward broke up with Bella and moved away from Forks because he wanted to protect Bella and save her soul.

## Which Way?

Every country, culture, community and individual in the world have their own unique meanings, values and ideas. Edward helps to show that the psychological impact of a person's spiritual view can be huge. At the simplest possible level, philosophy professor Tom Morris suggests that characters like Edward, Bella, Carlisle and everyone else on the planet can choose between two basic philosophical views: a *spiritual one* (theism) and a *non-spiritual one* (naturalism).

## The Non-Spiritual View

- Naturalism: a naturalistic worldview which considers life to be an impersonal reality
- What you are: a small, fleeting and unimportant speck in a huge physical universe
- Pessimistic outlook: spiritual energy does not exist in this view

- This is your life: you are born due to chance to exist briefly on earth, you live, you die, you disappear

Your life has no purpose:

- × No free will
- × No soul
- × No life after death
- × No links to higher forces, no meaning
- × No hope

## The Spiritual View

- Theism: a supernaturalistic worldview which considers that a supreme being or force exists
- What you are – an eternal and welcome addition to a spiritually rich and meaningful universe, meant to flourish forever
- Optimistic outlook – spiritual energy does exist
- This is your life – you are born from a divine creative source, you live, you die, you are transformed

Your life has purpose:

- ✓ A free will to search for meaning
- ✓ A soul
- ✓ Life after death
- ✓ Links with divine or eternal forces that give people meaning and happiness
- ✓ Hope

Well? As you have surely figured out, not only are these two views totally different to each other, the psychological implications are massive. After doing a bit of 'soul-searching', so to speak, Bella eventually favors the spiritual view, the one that promotes hope and happiness: 'I could see all the way into his soul. It seemed silly that this fact – the existence of his soul – had ever been in question, even if he was a vampire. He had the most beautiful soul' (*Breaking Dawn*, p22). The dismal *non*-spiritual view, by contrast, makes you want to curl up somewhere in a gutter and die, maybe. Why? Because life has no meaning or purpose whatsoever according to the naturalistic worldview. Yet, there is absolutely no doubt in the psychological literature that people feel and function far best when they have, or believe they have, some sort of control, direction and meaning in their lives. Knowing what is happening is much more preferable to being uninformed. Having a plan is much more effective than being unprepared. And being inspired by a higher purpose is far healthier and more powerful than the belief that there is no point to life at all.

As Edward illustrates so simply, elegantly and above all, powerfully, you can come from a very wealthy family, have lots of money, live in a big mansion, drive fast cars and wear nice clothes, but this does not guarantee a happy life if that life lacks spiritual meaning. As Edward tells Bella after she saved him from suicide in this ultimate love statement: 'I cannot be without you . . . You will always be the most beautiful thing in my world' (*New Moon*, p518–519).

## The Volturi's Void

What would a soulless world be like to live in? Imagine a community, city or country that possesses considerable military influence, material wealth, expert knowledge, powerful laws, a teeming population, fine housing and adequate food. Are individuals in such a society happier and better off? All these features are present in the Volturi Empire. Only spiritual direction is lacking. An existential interpretation of the Volturi, however, reveals some disturbing psychological results.

## Jane Executes Pain

Consider Jane, a prominent Volturi guard. She has a high-ranking social status, supernatural abilities and remarkable physical strength. Her unique talent is the ability to inflict extreme physical pain on others just by thinking about it. As such, Aro asks Jane to try out her pain-projecting 'gift' on Bella.

> 'Jane, dear?' . . .
> Little Jane smiled up happily at Aro. 'Yes, Master?' . . .
> 'I was wondering, my dear one, if Bella is immune to you.'
> (*New Moon*, p474)

Of course, as Twilight fans know, this adventure reveals that Bella is immune to Jane's torture. Edward, however, is not so lucky. He writhes in excruciating pain on the floor as Jane punishes his pleas and protests. Is Jane the free and powerful warrior that she thinks she is? Not according to compelling scientific evidence in psychology.

## Absolutely Shocking

Stanley Milgram's experiment *Obedience to Authority: An Experimental View* is one of the most famous works in psychology and its findings astonished the world. His experiments involved asking subjects to give a person strong electric shocks (subjects in the experiment were unaware that the shocks were not real, and that the targets of the shocks were just actors pretending to be in pain). Just as Aro asked Jane to inflict physical pain on Bella, Milgram's research found that when instructed by an authority figure dressed in uniform (a white laboratory coat), a majority of people were willing to administer lethal electric shocks to others. This experiment, which has been replicated around the world, showed that you don't have to be a sadistic monster to torture people. Many ordinary people will obey authority, even if they disagree with what they are told to do.

A main reason why many people continued to give the electric shocks was because they believed it would have been 'impolite' to go against the wishes of the experimenter. *The desire to please authority was more powerful than moral forces and the volunteer's cries of pain.* To reduce their feelings of guilt for inflicting pain strong enough to kill people, Milgram found that the shock-givers developed some interesting coping mechanisms:

- 'I was just following orders' was a common reason. As such, the shock-givers shifted moral responsibility to the leader, which is a common defense used in war crime trials.
- People focused on the 'technical' aspects of their duties.
- Shock-givers chose to believe that their action would benefit 'a greater cause'.
- Pain-producers devalued the victim by thinking things like: 'If they are too stupid to answer correctly, they deserve to be punished.'

This research evidence proved that if an authority – like the Volturi – demands it, people will be cruel. This means that vampires, who obey authority blindly, like Jane, may not have the free choice that they think they do.

For example, soldiers in real life are trained to fight for 'honor' and 'duty', to eliminate the enemy, and to 'always follow orders', or else pay the ultimate price – a possible death penalty. Although guards like Jane think they are free agents, they have been trained to be obedient weapons of destruction. In the Twilight series, this is exactly what the nomad vampire Garrett tried to point out about the Volturi vampires: 'Their guard is just a mindless weapon, a tool in their masters' quest for dominion' (*Breaking Dawn,* p667). The Volturi are much like a Milgram experiment – a spiritually empty and dangerous force.

## A Dead Life

Another danger of spiritually empty societies like that of the Volturi is that its members are much easier to brainwash. A great 20th-century American thinker, Eric Hoffer, argued that people get swept up by political movements to escape responsibility and misery in their lives. In other words, individuals such as Jane, Alec, Demetri and Felix are compelled to join pressure groups like Nazism, terrorism or Volturism because their own individual lives are so spiritually empty. Spiritual hunger drives people to dump their old unhappy identities so that they can change their lives and become part of something new, great and glorious. That's why manipulative mass movement leaders offer hope and promise to others. In the Twilight Saga, the Volturi leader Aro tries to tempt Edward, Alice – and even Bella – to join his dominion:

> 'Your talent would be an excellent addition to our little company . . . Would you perhaps be interested in joining with us? . . . Imagine the possibilities' (*New Moon*, p466–467).

If individuals are unhappy with who they are, it is much easier to lose an unwanted identity inside a pressure group where individuals do not matter, only the 'great cause' matters. The meaningless and miserable experience of individual life is instantly transformed into group pride, purpose, devotion, and strength. This is something that the Volturi army presence surely conveys:

> They came in rigid, formal formation. They moved together, but it was not a march; they flowed in perfect synchronicity from the trees – a dark, unbroken shape . . . Their progress was slow but deliberate, with no hurry, no tension, no anxiety. It was the pace of the invincible (*Breaking Dawn*, p632–633)

A glorious end justifies any means, and new believers will do horrible things to others for a grand cause and to protect their new paradise. If present life is considered worthless and the belief in a movement is great, people will be happy to die for it. Nazi officers, kamikaze pilots, terrorists, suicide bombers, and Volturi soldiers are no longer individuals, but loyal and unrecognizable members of a fanatical group.

These days, more than ever, many people seem to have empty, aimless, and meaningless lives. Some people try to fill their lives with too much pleasure, aggression or greed. They eat too much, obsess about money, or hate everyone. Some people get hooked on fashion fads, movie stars, the internet, retail therapy or gangs. Young people get drunk every weekend, older people panic when they retire, and many people just withdraw from life completely, sinking themselves into passive entertainment, like watching TV every night. People are increasingly hurting themselves, others, society, or all three. The psychiatrist Dr Victor Frankl calls this spiritually empty pattern of 'depression, addiction, and aggression' the *mass neurotic triad*.

Modern life, according to Bob Moorehead's description, is a bit like a funeral for the soul:

> We have taller buildings but shorter tempers, wider Freeways, but narrower viewpoints. We spend more, but have less, we buy more, but enjoy less. We have bigger houses and smaller families, more conveniences, but less time . . . We've conquered the atom, but not our prejudice . . . These are the times of fast foods and slow digestion, big men and small character, steep profits and shallow relationships.
>
> We've cleaned up the air, but polluted the soul.

As the Volturi's spiritual void in the Twilight books suggests, individuals who lack higher meaning and purpose in life are easy prey and can lose themselves to social pressures. But not individuals like Carlisle. He decided to be a better vampire, a vegetarian feeder, and to help, not harm, humans. Carlisle affirmed his spiritual needs, which could not be fulfilled in a spiritually empty Volturi cult.

## Never Lose the Spark

To sparkle, you first need a spark. Something or someone that fires you up, that makes you come alive inside, that lights up your soul. A shy and lonely Bella found love. From being a girl whose life was 'devoid of belief' (*New Moon*, p36), love enlightened Bella to see far into Edward's 'most beautiful soul' (*Breaking Dawn*, p22). Edward found Bella who believed in him always. This helped him to find his soul-mate at last, after spending more than 100 years alone. Jacob, who at first denied his link to Quileute spiritual power, finally stepped out into the sunlight (the social spotlight) as an Alpha – a brave leader of wolves. What do these Twilight experiences have in common? Each Twilight character found a 'spark' of inspiration that set their spiritual paths ablaze and empowered them to sparkle brightly and spiritually.

To sparkle, you first need a spark, which comes from fire. Fire is the only element that can ignite matter and has no limits – it cannot be contained. Fire is not a fixed or fluid element like earth or water, but a blaze of shape-shifting possibilities. Maybe your spark relates to determination, imagination, creativity, passion, courage, love, the spirit, or a feeling that you are connected to the great power of the universe. Once, in the Twilight Saga, Edward's 'doubt was suddenly replaced with a blazing determination' (*Twilight*, p397). Willpower was the spark, a hot and high-energy vibration.

Whatever you do, do not underestimate the power of a tiny spark. In the 19th century, the great writer Taras Shevchenko – the William Shakespeare of Ukraine – once wrote about a spark that lingered on long after enemy soldiers burned down a village and destroyed the lives of the local people:

*A lone spark of that great fire*
*Smoldered, did not perish*
*Amid the burnt-out embers*
*The spark smoldered on . . . it waited.*

This 'fire hidden deeply', Shevchenko goes on, was the 'spark of freedom' deep inside the soul. In other words, the desire for oppressed people to be free keeps living on in the spirit and can never die. It will smolder, waiting for the right moment to burn bright and foster a free future.

This important 'inner spark' idea is also echoed in modern culture in many places, even in Katy Perry's *Firework* song:

*You're a firework,*
*Come on, show 'em what you're worth.*
*Make 'em go 'Oh, oh, oh!'*
*As you shoot across the sky-y-y.*

The spark that makes the inner spirit sparkle, just as Edward shines and sparkles in the sun, has the utmost survival and health value according to the psychological literature. Spirituality is considered to be a worthy psychotherapeutic intervention for a range of cultures. Spiritual coping practices solve problems, strengthen coping, increase mental health and psychological well-being, ease the negative emotional impact of violence, and reduce feelings of hopelessness, depression and anxiety (Thomas, 2001). Spiritual coping involves developing a personal and meaningful relationship with a higher power and developing a sense of purpose or meaning in one's life. This can include prayer, seeking support from spiritual leaders, believing in a benevolent higher power, having a positive relationship with God, or attending a place of worship. An important study designed by Dr Arnette and colleagues at the Emory University School of Medicine found that spiritual coping strategies helped people who were living in violent family situations. It decreased their depression, suicidal behavior, anxiety, low self-esteem, and feelings of helplessness and hopelessness. Such strategies protected people from stress, reduced psychological distress, improved mental and spiritual well-being, and helped individuals find meaning in their lives.

It doesn't matter what kind of spark you use to inspire yourself or keep your spirit alive. Maybe you desire to ignite your dreams, or find your intuitive glow. Burn with love or be a risk-taking trail-blazer. Reduce your suffering to ashes or feel the fireworks of happiness. If you develop a 'spark' inside your soul, you have the power to sparkle spiritually and light every star in your heaven. One thing is for sure, as the Twilight Saga's sparkling vampires suggest and Ferdinand's inspiring quote asserts: 'The most powerful weapon on earth is the human soul on fire.'

# Shine with Insight

> Everything was so CLEAR.
> Sharp. Defined . . . Brilliant.
> (*Breaking Dawn*, p357)

The first time Bella sees the same world around her with new vampire eyes, everything looks different – sharp and clear.

Just as Bella perceived her surroundings as a 'brilliant' place, now *you* have developed the power to see the hidden psychological brilliance of the Twilight Saga more clearly, sharply and deeply than ever before.

Bella, Edward, Jacob and other Twilight favorites are our awesome friends-forever who tell a fascinating psychological story about dreams, senses, love, risk, suffering, choices, and a sparkling inner force. With help from the Twilight world, just a few of the exciting psychological insights, knowledge and Skills4Life that you have gained from this book relate to:

- The unconscious mind and the power of dreams
- The intuitive sense and how it guides you
- The psychological secrets of true love
- The Twilight Saga's best self-control strategies
- Knowledge and skills to survive depression, suicide and anxiety
- How to increase feelings of authentic happiness
- Soul-loving psychology skills

### What's *Your* Next Life?

You don't have "to die" in the flesh or become a blood-drinker to experience a shiny new life. You know yourself better than anyone. And you have a choice to do something different and brilliant today to transform your life – and light up the night like a shooting star. We all have special gifts inside, incredible psychological strengths. And as Bella, Edward, Jacob and their fine and fearless friends help to show time and time again, you have an opportunity to develop *yours*. Maybe it is time to do something really fantastic for yourself and make your next life, the one starting now, the most freakin' spectacular journey you will ever be on. Psychologically speaking, maybe you have reached a twilight time in your life right now and feel ready to explore your inner night, embrace your new moon experience, and master the things that eclipse the bright light of the breaking dawn that awaits you. As the Twilight Saga shows, no matter who you are, where you are, or how you are in your life at the moment, you have the power to change your world, realize your greatest dream, and take positive action to experience a dazzling psychological adventure that begins with just one delicious and daring... bite.

# Meet the Author

Dr Julie-Anne Sykley is full-blood Ukrainian – a descendant of the dark, wild places of East Europe. Hey, that's *vampire* country! Vampire myths originate in Slavic folklore, for the winters are long and cold here, and the landscape raw and rugged. In fact, the word *vampire* derives from the Slavic root *pi*, which means to 'drink' or 'drain'.

Julie-Anne is also a fully qualified Australian psychologist with more than 20 years' professional experience helping people. From inner-city Sydney to the remote Territory outback, she has assisted young people, adults, offenders, prisoners and traditional Aboriginal people to deal with a wide range of mental health issues. Julie-Anne is keen to promote mental health skills and increase people's power to deal with emotional problems, especially depression, suicide, and anxiety. This is why she wrote this book for you!

Julie-Anne currently resides in Far North Australia where she lives with cyclones, crocodiles, her partner Steffanko (a Croatian vampire) and a bright-red parrot named Ruby.

Beware! If Julie-Anne was ever turned into a Twilight-style

vampire, her 'gift' would be a non-stop crazy 'super-humor'.

## What does the cover design mean?

The *apple* – a symbol of 'knowledge', 'immortality' and 'temptation' used in the Twilight Saga – is submerged in water. The underwater image points to this book's exploration of powerful psychological processes contained within the Twilight Saga as well as the fascinating and forbidden thoughts submerged in our own minds. Inside the mind, many thoughts, ideas and secrets dwell deep somewhere. Some thoughts lurk unseen, hidden far beneath our awareness – below the surface of the water, so to speak.

## Thank you!

I really hope this book helps you, empowers you or inspires you somehow. If you really liked something in this book or didn't like things in this book, do share your thoughts online and recommend the book to others. *Your* comments are important and will assist other people on their quest for knowledge and support, health and happiness, love and adventure.

If you think something in this book will really benefit others, feel free to share it and Like, Tweet or Digg it.

Please leave comments or feedback on Amazon.com.

# References


Aanstoos, C. Serlin, I., and Greening, T. (2000). A History of Division 32 (Humanistic Psychology) of the American Psychological Association. In D. Dewsbury (Ed.) *Unification through Division: Histories of the divisions of the American Psychological Association*, Vol. V. Washington, DC: American Psychological Association.

American Foundation for Suicide Prevention (2011). www.afsp.org/index.cfm (March 30, 2011).

American Psychiatric Association (APA) (2005). Diagnostic and Statistical Manual of Mental Disorders: Fourth Edition – Text Revision (DSM IV-TR). Washington: APA.

Anxiety. www.getselfhelp.co.uk/anxiety.htm (March 30, 2011).

Argyle M (2002). *The Psychology of Happiness*. Routledge.

Arnette, Natalie C., Mascaro, Nathan., Santana, M. Carmen., Davis, Shane., and Kaslow, Nadine J. (2007). Enhancing Spiritual Well-Being Among Suicidal African American Female Survivors of Intimate Partner Violence. *Journal of Clinical Psychology*, 63(10), 909–924.

Baba Yaga: Black Crone Goddess. 'Black, red, and white are the three colors associated with personal transformation'. In Dark Goddesses. www.dutchie.org/Tracy/goddess/baba.html (May 13, 2011).

Baba Yaga. www.blueroebuck.com/babayaga.html (March 30, 2011).

Baba Yaga and the Cycles of Death and Initiation. Mills, Alice (2005) (Chief Consultant) *Mythology: Myths, Legends and Fantasies*. Sydney: Hodder.

Baba Yaha. Malko, Roman. In Fabulous creatures of Ukrainian folklore – is there more to them than just superstition and old beliefs? www.wumag.kiev.ua/index2.php?param=pgs20043/70 (March 30, 2011).

Bates, S (2006). How the eagle chooses her mate. *Smoke Signal Newsletter* 10 (7). http://www. Manataka.org/page1989.html. Cited in Garnier R. and Yapko M.D. Empowering Lisa: The Power of Metaphor for a Depressed and Suicidal Teen, pp139–150. In Burns, G.W. (Ed.) (2010) *Happiness, Healing, Enhancement: Casebook Collection for Applying Positive Psychology in Therapy*. New Jersey: John Wiley and Sons.

Beck, A.T., Brown, G., Berchick, R., Stewart, B., and Steer, R. (1990). Relationship between hopelessness and ultimate suicide: A replication with psychiatric outpatients. *American Journal of Psychiatry*, 147, 190–195.

Beck, A.T., and Steer, R. (1993). *Beck Hopelessness Scale Manual*. San Antonio: Psychological Corporation.

Beck, A.T., Steer, R.A., Kovacs, M., and Garrison, B. (1985). Hopelessness and eventual suicide: A ten-year prospective study of patients hospitalized with suicidal ideation. *American Journal of Psychiatry*, 142, 559–563.

Beck, A.T., Weissman, A., Lester, D., and Trexler, L. (1974). The measurement of pessimism: The Hopelessness Scale. *Journal of Consulting and Clinical Psychology*, 42, 861–865.

Beck A.T., Rush A.J., Shaw B.F. and Emery G. (1979) *Cognitive Therapy of Depression*. New York: The Guilford Press.

Benne and Sheats (1948). Group Roles. In http://www.speaking .pitt.edu/student/groups/smallgrouproles.html (June 5, 2010).

Bennett-Goleman, T. (2001) *Emotional Alchemy*. London: Rider.

Bennett-Levy (2009). Evidence-Based CBT for Depression Course. Byron Bay, New South Wales: Northern Rivers University Department of Rural Health.

Beyond Blue Suicide Statistics, Australia. www.beyondblue.org. au/index.aspx?link_id=105.898&oid=888 (March 30, 2011).

Beyondblue: The national depression initiative. Anxiety Disorders Brochure (2009) (12/09).

Beyondblue: The national depression initiative. Dealing with Anxiety Disorders (2009). Youthbeyondblue Fact sheet 2

(10/09).

Beyondblue: The national depression initiative. Depression in Young People (2009). Youthbeyondblue Fact Sheet 1 (10/09).

Beyondblue: The national depression initiative. What causes depression? (2009). Youthbeyondblue Fact Sheet 3 (10/09).

Black Dog Institute. Fact Sheets on Positive Psychology. Fact Sheets on Happiness. Prince of Wales Hospital: Randwick NSW 2031. www.blackdoginstitute.org.au/factsheets/index .cfm (April 5, 2011).

Boss, M. and Craig, E. In Lewis, J.R. (1995) *The Dream Encyclopedia*. New York: Gale Research Inc.

Bourne, E.J. (1995). *The Anxiety and Phobia Workbook* (Second Edition). Oakland: New Harbinger Publications.

Bowes, S. (1999). *Life Magic: The Power of Positive Witchcraft*. Sussex: The Ivy Press Ltd.

Brandon, N. Cited in Flora, Carlin. The Pursuit of Happiness: Has the happiness frenzy of the past few years left you sad and anxious? Herein we report the surest ways to find well-being. Published on January 01, 2009; reviewed November 03, 2010. www.psychologytoday.com/articles/200812/the-pursuit-happiness (April 19, 2011).

Breckler S.J., Olson J.M., and Wiggins E.C. (2006). *Social Psychology Alive*. Belmont, CA: Thomson Wadsworth.

Bridge, S. Adapted from Dr Simon Bridge. *Toughin' It Out*, www.kirinaran.com (April 14, 2005).

Bryant F.B., Veroff J. (2006). *Savoring: A New Model of Positive Experience*. Lawrence Erlbaum Associates.

Burns, G.W. Now I Can Get On with Life: Pleasure, Engagement, and Meaning in a Case of Major Depression, pp127–138. In Burns, G.W. (Ed.) (2010) *Happiness, Healing, Enhancement: Casebook Collection for Applying Positive Psychology in Therapy*. New Jersey: John Wiley and Sons.

Capriles, E. (2006). Beyond Mind II: Further Steps to a Metatranspersonal Philosophy and Psychology. San

Francisco, California: *The International Journal of Transpersonal Studies* [2], 24:5–44.

CBT (Cognitive Behaviour Techniques) for Addiction. Leader's Guide: Functional Analysis/The 5 Ws. www.unodc.org/ddt-training/treatment/.../1.../VolB_M3_Guide.ppt. (October 31, 2010).

Centre for Clinical Interventions (CCI) in Western Australia. Mastering Anxiety: Letting Go of Worries. www.cci.health.wa.gov.au/ (June 24, 2011).

Chinen, Allan B. The Emergence of Transpersonal Psychiatry. In Scotton, Bruce W., Chinen, Allan B. and Battista, John R. (Eds.) (1996) *Textbook of Transpersonal Psychiatry and Psychology*. New York: Basic Books.

Cognitive Behaviour Therapy Self-Help Resources: GET Self-Help. 'Distancing or Defusing from Thoughts: What is Mindfulness'. www.getselfhelp.co.uk/freedownloads.htm. (October 31, 2010).

sColin, Didier (2000) *Dictionary of Symbols, Myths and Legends*. London: Hachette Illustrated.

Csikzentmihalyi, M. (1997) *Finding Flow: The Psychology of Engagement with Everyday Life*. Basic Books

Csikzentmihalyi, M. (1991) *Flow: The Psychology of Optimal Experience*. Harper Perennial.

Daley and Marlatt (2007). In Lintzeris, N., Dunlop, A. and Thornton, D. (1999) Getting Through Alcohol Withdrawal: A guide for people trying to stop alcohol use. Melbourne: Turning Point Alcohol and Drug Centre Inc.

Davies, J. (2000) *A Manual of Mental Health Care in General Practice*. Canberra: Commonwealth Department of Health and Aged Care.

De Becker, G. (1998) *The Gift of Fear: Survival Signals That Protect Us from Violence.* Random House Publishing Group.

Devine, M. (2011). Fairytale Princess: Will and Kate's Royal Wedding. *The Cairns Weekend Post*. April 30–May 1, 2011, p1.

Diamond, Stephen (4 March, 2010). Clinical Despair: Science, Psychotherapy and Spirituality in the Treatment of Depression. http://www.psychologytoday.com/blog/evil-deeds/201103/clinical-despair-science-psychotherapy-and-spirituality-in-the-treatment-depr (March 17, 2011).

Diener, E. (1994). Assessing subjective well-being: Progress and opportunities. *Social Indicators Research*, 31, 103–157.

Diener, E., Horowitz, J. and Emmons, R. (1985). Happiness of the very wealthy. *Social Indicators Research*, 16, 263–274.

Dombeck, M. and Wells-Moran, J. (Updated March 5, 2010). Coping Strategies and Defense Mechanisms: Mature Defenses (July 3, 2006). www.mentalhelp.net/ (March 21, 2011).

Dylan, B. (1964). Singer/Songwriter for 'Take me disappearing . . . crazy sorrow'. Lyrics from *Mr. Tambourine Man*. Warner Bros. www.bobdylan.com/songs/mr-tambourine-man (April 12, 2011).

Eason, C. (2002) *Ancient Wisdom*. Bath: Parragon Books.

Einstein, A. 'The intuitive mind is a sacred gift'. www.greatest-inspirational-quotes.com/intuition-quotes.html (March 4, 2011).

Ellison, C.W. (1983). Spiritual well-being: Conceptualization and measurement. *Journal of Psychology and Theology*, 11, 330–340.

Emmons R. (2007). *Thanks! How the New Science of Gratitude Can Make You Happier*. Houghton Mifflin.

Ferdinand. 'The most powerful weapon on earth is the human soul on fire'. Fochhttp://www.quotegarden.com/soul.html (Accessed April 5, 2011)

Flora, Carlin. The Pursuit of Happiness. Published on January 01, 2009; reviewed November 03, 2010. www.psychology-today .com/articles/200812/the-pursuit-happiness (April 19, 2011).

Fontana, David, Slack, Ingrid and Treacy, Martin (Eds) (2005) Transpersonal Psychology: Meaning and Developments. *Transpersonal Psychology Review Special Issue*. Leicester: British

Psychological Society.

*Forests of the Vampire* (1999) London: Duncan Baird Publishers, 1999. In The Slavic Origins of Vampire Myth. www.suite101.com/content/the-slavic-origins-of-vampire-myth (April 11, 2011).

Frank, Anne. 'I soothe my conscience . . . in her heart'. http://classiclit.about.com/od/frankanne/a/aa_afrankquote.htm (April 5, 2011).

Frankl, V. In Heidegger, M. Cited in Magill, F.N. and Rodriguez, J. (Eds) (1996) *International Encyclopedia of Psychology*. London: Fitzroy Dearborn Publishers.

Frankl, Viktor (2004) *Man's Search for Meaning*. Random House: London.

Frankl, Viktor. 'Meaning must be found and cannot be given'. http://webspace.ship.edu/cgboer/frankl.html (March 4, 2011).

Freire, Teresa. From Vulnerability to Skillfulness: Leisure and Positive Intervention in Therapy with Adolescents, pp100–112. In Burns, G.W. (Ed.) (2010) *Happiness, Healing, Enhancement: Casebook Collection for Applying Positive Psychology in Therapy*. New Jersey: John Wiley and Sons.

Freud, A. (1948) *The Ego and the Mechanisms of Defence*. London: The Hogarth Press.

Freud, S. (translated by Joyce Crick) (1990) *The Interpretation of Dreams*. Oxford: Oxford University Press.

Freud, S. In Butler-Bowndon, T. (2007) *50 Psychology Classics*. London: Nicholas Brealey Publishing.

Freud, S. In Heidegger, M. Cited in Magill, F.N. and Rodriguez, J. (Eds) (1996) *International Encyclopedia of Psychology*. London: Fitzroy Dearborn Publishers.

Galanter, E. In Heidegger, M. Cited in Magill, F.N. and Rodriguez, J. (Eds) (1996) *International Encyclopedia of Psychology*. London: Fitzroy Dearborn Publishers.

Garnier, R. and Yapko, M.D. Empowering Lisa, pp139–150. In Burns, G.W. (Ed.) (2010) *Happiness, Healing, Enhancement:*

*Casebook Collection for Applying Positive Psychology in Therapy*. New Jersey: John Wiley and Sons.

Glikin-Gusinsky, A. Slavic Origins of Vampire Myth.

http://www.suite101.com/content/the-slavic-origins-of-vampire-myth-a306789 (Nov 9, 2010)

Glasser, W. *'We almost always have choices'*. http://www.glasser-northeast.com/index.php?option=com_content&task=view&id=58&Itemid=107 (June 7, 2011).

Glasser, W. (1999) *Choice Theory: A New Psychology of Personal Freedom*. New York: Harper Perennial.

Goleman, D. (1996) *Emotional Intelligence*. Bloomsbury: London.

Granger, J. (2009) *Spotlight: A Close-Up Look at the Artistry and Meaning of Stephenie Meyer's Twilight Saga*. Zossima Press.

Graves, R. 'Intuition is the supra-logic . . . to the answer'. http://thinkexist.com/quotations/intuition/ (June 30, 2011).

Grof, Stanislav and Grof, Christina (Eds) (1989) *Spiritual Emergency: When Personal Transformation Becomes a Crisis* (New Consciousness Reader) Los Angeles: J.P. Tarcher.

Grof, Stanislav (1998) *The Cosmic Game: Explorations of the Frontiers of Human Consciousness*. Albany, New York: State University of New York (SUNY) Press.

Hare, R.D. (1991) *The Hare Psychopathy Checklist-Revised Manual*. New York: Multi-Health Systems.

Harlow, H. (1958). The Nature of Love. *American Psychologist*, 13, 573–685.

Harlow, H. http://psychclassics.yorku.ca/Harlow/love.htm (May 13, 2011).

Harris, Russell (2006). Embracing Your Demons: An Overview of Acceptance and Commitment Therapy. *Psychotherapy from Australia*. Vol. 12, No. 4, August, pp2–8.

Heidegger, M. Cited in Magill, F.N. and Rodriguez, J. (Eds) (1996) *International Encyclopedia of Psychology*. London: Fitzroy Dearborn Publishers.

Herzberg, F. In Heidegger, M. Cited in Magill, F.N. and

Rodriguez, J. (Eds) (1996) *International Encyclopedia of Psychology*. London: Fitzroy Dearborn Publishers.

Hill, P.C., and Pargament, K.I. (2003). Advances in the conceptualization and measurement of religion and spirituality: Implications for physical and mental health research. *American Psychologist*, 58, 64–74.

Hoffer, E. (1980) *The True Believer: Thoughts on the Nature of Mass Movements*. Chicago: Time-Life Books.

Hoffer, E. Eric Hoffer. The True Believer: Thoughts on the Nature of Mass Movements, pp152–155. In Butler-Bowdon, T. (2007) *50 Psychology Classics*. London: Nicholas Brealey Publishing.

Hogan C. and Champagne, D.W. *MBTI Styles of Communication*. Paper presented at 1995 Banyule City Council MBTI Team Workshop, Melbourne.

'How to be great! Describes a hero's character traits: Courage and strength; Honesty; Kindness and generosity; Risk-taking'. *Psychology Today* Staff, reviewed November 24, 2010. www.psychologytoday.com/articles/199511/how-be-great (April 1, 2011).

'Inner essence of a person'. Nagai-Jacobson, M.G. and Burckhardt, M.A. (1989) Spirituality: cornerstone of holistic nursing practice. *Holistic Nursing Practice* 3 (3), 69–77.

James, W. In Heidegger, M. Cited in Magill, F.N. and Rodriguez, J. (Eds) (1996) *International Encyclopedia of Psychology*. London: Fitzroy Dearborn Publishers.

Jung, C. In Heidegger, M. Cited in Magill, F.N. and Rodriguez, J. (Eds) (1996) *International Encyclopedia of Psychology*. London: Fitzroy Dearborn Publishers.

Jung, C. 'The dream is specifically the utterance of the unconscious.' The Practical Use of Dream Analysis (1934). In C.W. 16: *The Practice of Psychotherapy*. p317 www.netreach.net/~nhojem/dreamq.htm (March 4, 2011).

Kahneman D., Diener E., Schwarz, N. (Eds) (2003). Well--Being: The Foundations of Hedonic Psychology. Russell Sage

Foundation Publications.

Kashdan, T. (2009) *Curious? Discover the Missing Ingredient to a Fulfilling Life*. New York: HarperCollins Books.

Kekule, F.A. In Lewis, J.R. (1995) *The Dream Encyclopedia*. New York: Gale Research Inc.

Keyes, C.L.M., Haidt, J. (Eds) (2003). Flourishing: Positive Psychology and the Life Well-Lived. American Psychological Association.

Klein, S. (2006) *The Science of Happiness*. Avalon.

Knight, Sirona (1998) *Celtic Spirituality*. Berkeley, CA: The Crossing Press.

Koenig, H.G. (2001). Religion and medicine II: Religion, mental health, and related behaviors. *International Journal of Psychiatry in Medicine*, 31, 97–109.

Krebs Hirsh, S. and Kummerow, J. (1989) *Life Types*. New York: Warner Books.

Kubler-Ross, E. 'People are like stained-glass windows' quote.
www.quotiki.com/quotes/10120 (June 24, 2011)

Lajoie, D.H. and Shapiro, S.I. (1992). Definitions of transpersonal psychology: The first twenty-three years. *Journal of Transpersonal Psychology*, Vol. 24.

Layard, R. (2006) *Happiness: Lessons from a New Science*. Penguin.

Ledbetter, M.F., Smith, L.A., Vosler-Hunter, W.L., and Fischer, J.D. (1991). An evaluation of the research and clinical usefulness of the Spiritual Well-Being Scale. *Journal of Psychology and Theology*, 19, 49–55.

Le Roux, R. and de Klerk-Wyer, R. (2008) *Emotional Intelligence: A Workbook for Our Wellbeing*. Human and Rousseau.

Lewis, J.R. (1995) *The Dream Encyclopedia*. New York: Gale Research Inc.

Linley, P. and Burns, G.W. Strengthspotting: Finding and Developing Client Resources in the Management of Intense Anger, pp1–14. In Burns, G.W. (Ed.) (2010) *Happiness, Healing, Enhancement: Casebook Collection for Applying Positive*

*Psychology in Therapy*. New Jersey: John Wiley and Sons.

Lintzeris, N., Dunlop, A. and Thornton, D. (1999) Getting Through Alcohol Withdrawal: A guide for people trying to stop alcohol use. Melbourne: Turning Point Alcohol and Drug Centre Inc.

'Lisovyk'. Forest Spirit. *Encyclopedia of Ukraine*. http://www.encyclopediaofukraine.com (April 5, 2011).

'Lisovyk'. Slavic Fairies. Wikipedia, the free encyclopedia. taggedwiki.zubiaga.org/.../2188413120829607e4a138b18c1b8507 (April 5, 2011).

Lohmann, Raychelle Cassada (October 30, 2010), MS. 'Teens and the deadly games that they play.' http://www.psychology-today.com/blog/teen-angst/201010/the-deadly-games-teens-play-0) (March 7, 2011).

Lubomirsky, S. (2007) *The How of Happiness: A Scientific Approach to Getting the Life You Want*. Penguin Press H.C.

Lykken, D. Twin Studies. http://dlibrary.acu.edu.au/research/ageing/thot/thotarchives/thot2003&4/thot04dec03.html (June 1, 2011).

Mackay, C. *No Enemies*. In Untermeyer, L. (Ed.) (1973) *The Golden Treasury of Poetry*. New York: Golden Press.

Magill, F.N. and Rodriguez, J. (Eds) (1996) *International Encyclopedia of Psychology*. London: Fitzroy Dearborn Publishers.

Maier, S. In Weiss, R. (1999) Sixth sense: it's not all in the mind. *The Age* (Melbourne), 7 May 1999, pp86–87.

Malko, R. Fabulous creatures of Ukrainian folklore. http://www.wumag.kiev.ua (April 5, 2011).

Marrianna Marinda (2011). Gnostic Symbolism in 'Harry Potter' . . . or rather, 'Twilight'. Message posted May 30, 2011. http://groups.yahoo.com/group/harrypotterforseekers/message/4063 (July 1, 2011).

Maslow, A. In Heidegger, M. Cited in Magill, F.N. and Rodriguez, J. (Eds) (1996) *International Encyclopedia of Psychology*. London:

Fitzroy Dearborn Publishers.

Maslow, A. (1976) *The Farther Reaches of Human Nature*. London: Penguin.

McGorry, Patrick. In Rose, Danny. Suicide Taboo Taking Lives. *The Weekend Post*, March 27, 2010, p38.

McMahon, T. 'Yes, risk-taking is inherently failure prone' quote. www.quotes.net/authors/Tim+McMahon (June 21, 2011).

Meyer, S. (2006) *Twilight*. London: Atom Books.

Meyer, S. (2007) *New Moon*. London: Atom Books.

Meyer, S. (2007) *Eclipse*. London: Atom Books.

Meyer, S. (2008) *Breaking Dawn*. London: Atom Books.

Meyer, S. (2009) *The Twilight Journals*. New York: Little, Brown and Company.

Milgram, S. (1974) *Obedience to Authority*. New York: HarperCollins.

Milgram, S. 'Stanley Milgram. Obedience to Authority: An Experimental View, pp198–203. In Butler-Bowdon, T. (2007) *50 Psychology Classics*. London: Nicholas Brealey Publishing.

Milkman, H. (October 25, 2009). Can risk-taking and thrill-seeking evoke altered states? www.psychologytoday .com/blog/better-dope/200910/(March 7, 2011).

Miller, W.R., and Thoresen, C.E. (2003). Spirituality, religion, and health: An emerging research field. *American Psychologist*, 58, 24–35.

Mindfulness. Centre for Clinical Interventions. www.cci.health. wa.gov.au/docs/ACF1097.pdf (March 30, 2011).

Moorehead, B. The Paradox of Our Time. http://www.trans 4mind.com/counterpoint/moorehead.shtml (June 5, 2011).

Morris, T. (1999) *Philosophy for Dummies*. Foster City, CA: IDG Books Worldwide Inc.

Moss, S. (1989) *Jungian Typology: Myers Briggs and Personality*. Melbourne: Collins Dove.

Mudrack, P. and Farrell, G. (1995). An examination of functional role behavior and its consequences for individuals in group settings. *Small Group Research*, 26, 542–571.

Mudrack and Farrell (1995). Group Roles. In *Communication Skills: The Ways Informal Roles Influence Groups and Teams*. http://www.ag.iastate.edu/centers/ftcsc/media/ways.pdf (June 5, 2011).

Murphy, P.E., Ciarrocchi, J.W., Piedmont, R.L., Cheston, S., Peyrot, M., and Fitchett, G. (2000). The relation of religious belief and practices, depression, and hopelessness in persons with clinical depression. *Journal of Consulting and Clinical Psychology*, 68, 1102–1106.

Myers, D. (2002) *Intuition: Its Power and Perils*. R.R. Donnelly and Sons.

Myers-Briggs, I. In Moss, S. (1989) *Jungian Typology: Myers Briggs and Personality*. Melbourne: Collins Dove.

National Aboriginal Community Controlled Organisation (NACCHO) (1997) *What is Mental Health? How Indigenous People See Mental Health*. Brisbane: Queensland Health.

Niemiec R.M. and Wedding, D. 'Twilight is a positive psychology film: Edward and self-control' (Posted November 24, 2009). http://www.wellsphere.com/happiness-article/8216-twilight-8217-as-a-positive-psychology-film-edward-and-self-control/894617. Positive Psychology At The Movies: Using Films to Build Virtues and Character Strengths, by Ryan M. Niemiec, Danny Wedding **from** *Self-Regulation on the Silver Screen* (March 17, 2011).

Nozedar, A. (2008) *Element Encyclopedia of Secret Signs and Symbols*. Barnes and Noble.

Office for National Statistics (2011) *Suicide rates in the United Kingdom, 2000–2009*. Statistical Bulletin. Crown.

Orloff, Judith (February 28, 2011). How to liberate yourself from negative emotions and create a positive life. Learn how to cope with our anger in a healthy way (March 17, 2011).

Perry, K. Fireworks Lyrics. www.metrolyrics.com/firework-lyrics-katy-perry.html (June 29, 2011).

Petersen, C. (2006) *A Primer in Positive Psychology*. Oxford University Press.

Petersen, C. (2004) *Character Strengths and Virtues: A Handbook and Classification*. Oxford University Press.

Phillips, C. and Kerrigan, M. (2003) *Forests of the Vampire: Slavic Myth*. Sterling Publishing.

Phillips, S.D. Waxing Like the Moon: Women Folk Healers in Rural Western Ukraine.

*Folklorica: Journal of the Slavic and East European Folkore Association. ISSN 1920-0242.*

Electronic article hosted by the Center for Digital Scholarship, University of Kansas Libraries. https://journals.ku.edu/index.php/folklorica/article/viewFile/3744/3583 (April 5, 2011).

Post, S., Neimark, J. (2007) *Why Good Things Happen to Good People*. Broadway.

Powell, T. (2010) *The Mental Health Handbook: A Cognitive Behavioural Approach* (Third Edition). Milton Keynes: UK.

Prisgrove, P. (1991) A Relapse Prevention Approach to Reducing Aggressive Behaviour, pp179–191. In Serious Violent Offenders: Sentencing, Psychiatry and Law Reform: Proceedings of a Conference 1991. Gerull, S. and Lucas, W. (1993) (Eds) Canberra: Australian Institute of Criminology.

Prochaska, J.O., DiClemente, C.C. and Norcross, J.C. (1992) In Search of How People Change: Applications to Addictive Behaviours. *American Psychologist*, 47 (9), 1102–1114.

Prodan, C. Can't Hide Your Lying Eyes. http://www.accessexcellence.org/WN/SUA14/liarliar.php (June 1, 2011).

Pynchon, Thomas. 'Let the vampire's creaking wing' quote.

www.goodreads.com/author/quotes/235.Thomas_Pynchon (June 21, 2011).

Quileute Creation Story with Wolves. www.quileutewolfpack.com/lapush/folklore.htm (March 29, 2011).

Quileute Legends. The Quileute Legend Website. http://www.

quileutes.com/quileute-legend/ (March 30, 2011).

Quileute Thunderbird Story. www.quileutewolfpack.com/lapush/folklore.htm (March 29, 2011).

Quileute Tribal Council (2009) *Native Village Youth and Education News: Quileute Welcome Whales*. May 1, 2010 (Vol. 1). www.nativevillage.org/Archives/2010 (March 30, 2011).

Ramsay Health Service (2010). Customer Service Orientation Module (November 2, 2010).

Reber, A.S., Allen, R. and Reber, E.S. (2009) *Penguin Dictionary of Psychology*. London: Penguin Books Ltd.

Rey, Joseph (2002) *More Than Just the Blues: Understanding Serious Teenage Problems*. Sydney: Simon & Schuster.

'Risk-taking' quotes. www.articlesnatch.com/Article/Youth-Quotes-Packed-With-Timeless-Wisdom/1515643#ixzz1GJ9BwTBZ (March 29, 2011).

Roosevelt, E. 'The purpose of life . . . and richer experience'. http://mental-health.families.com/blog/inspirational-quotes-from-inspirational-people (June 30, 2011).

Rossi, K.L. A Dream of Creative Menopause: A New Neuroscience of Brief Psychotherapy for Solving Puzzles of Biology and Psychology, pp252–266. In Burns, G.W. (Ed.) (2010) *Happiness, Healing, Enhancement: Casebook Collection for Applying Positive Psychology in Therapy*. New Jersey: John Wiley and Sons.

Rubin, Z. In Heidegger, M. Cited in Magill, F.N. and Rodriguez, J. (Eds) (1996) *International Encyclopedia of Psychology*. London: Fitzroy Dearborn Publishers.

Salsman, J.M., Brown, T.L., Brechting, E.H., and Carlson, C.R. (2005). The link between religion and spirituality and psychological adjustment: The mediating role of optimism and social support. *Personality and Social Psychology Bulletin*, 31, 522–535.

Scotton, Bruce W., Chinen, Allan B. and John R. Battista (Eds) (1996) *Textbook of Transpersonal Psychiatry and Psychology*. New York: Basic Books

Self-Testing for Depression Factsheet. www.blackdoginstitute.org.au/factsheets/index.cfm (March 27, 2011).

Seligman, M. Happiness. http://www.happylifeu.com/Quotes-on-Happiness.htm (April 5, 2011).

Seligman, M.E.P. (2003) *Authentic Happiness: Using the new positive psychology to realize your potential for lasting fulfillment.* New York: Free Press.

Seybold, K.S., and Hill, P.C. (2001). The role of religion and spirituality in mental and physical health. *Current Directions in Psychological Science*, 10, 21–24.

Shakespeare, William. 'To be or not to be'. *Hamlet*. In Bartlett, J. (1979) *A Complete Concordance to Shakespeare*. London: Macmillan Books.

Shakespeare, William (1595). 'With love's light wings'. *Romeo and Juliet*. In Bartlett, J. (1979) *A Complete Concordance to Shakespeare*. London: Macmillan Books.

Shevchenko, T. The Heretic. In Luckyj, G.S.N. (Ed.) (1961) *Taras Shevchenko Poems*. Molode Zyttia Press: Munich, Germany.

Slater, W., Hall, T.W., and Edwards, K.J. (2001). Measuring religion and spirituality: Where are we and where are we going? *Journal of Psychology and Theology*, 29, 4–21.

Slavic Origins of Vampire Myth. www.suite101.com/content/the-slavic-origins-of-vampire-myth (April 11, 2011).

Slavic Vampire Myth. http://en.wikipedia.org/wiki/Vampire_folklore_by_region

(Nov 9, 2010) Andrew Glikin-Gusinsky (April 11, 2011).

Snyder, C.R. (2005) *Handbook of Positive Psychology*. Oxford University Press.

Stoker, Bram (1992) *Dracula* (first published 1897). New York: Penguin Books Signet Classic.

Symptoms of Depression Factsheet. www.blackdoginstitute.org.au/factsheets/index.cfm (March 27, 2011).

Terjesen, A. and Terjesen, J. Carlisle: More Compassionate Than a Speeding Bullet? pp49–62. In Housel, R. and Wisnewski, J.

(Eds) (2009) *Twilight and Philosophy: Vampires, Vegetarians, and the Pursuit of Immortality*. New Jersey: John Wiley and Sons.

Thomas (2001). In Arnette, Natalie C., Mascaro, Nathan., Santana, M. Carmen., Davis, Shane., and Kaslow, Nadine J. (2007). Enhancing Spiritual Well-Being Among Suicidal African American Female Survivors of Intimate Partner Violence. *Journal of Clinical Psychology*, 63 (10), 909–924.

'Thrill-seeker dies after jumping off cliff'. News story Joe Meyer. *Columbia Daily Tribune*, Missouri. July 13, 2009. www.columbiatribune.com/news/2009/jul/13/jump-cliff-turns-fatal/ (March 15, 2011).

Transpersonal Psychology Definition. http://en.wikipedia.org/wiki/Transpersonal_psychology (June 1, 2011).

*Turning Point Alcohol and Drug Centre*. Lintzeris, N., Dunlop, A. and Thornton, D. (1999) Getting Through Alcohol Withdrawal: A guide for people trying to stop alcohol use. Melbourne: Turning Point Alcohol and Drug Centre Inc.

Tutu, Desmond (2007). In *Warcry: Faith and Culture* (Salvation Army Magazine). Vol. 126, No. 23, 16 June, 2007.

'Twilight' Definition. Wikipedia, the free encyclopedia. http://en.wikipedia.org/wiki/Twilight (March 31, 2011).

'Twilight' Symbolism. www.symbolism.org/writing/books/sp/4/page3.html (March 31, 2011).

'Vampire' (2001). www.encyclopedia.com/topic/Vampires.aspx. Encyclopedia of Occultism and Parapsychology (April 28, 2011).

Van der Kolk, Bessel A. (2005). Developmental Trauma Disorder: Toward a rational diagnosis for children with complex trauma histories. *Psychiatric Annals* 35:5, May 2005, pp391–408.

Vroom, V. In Heidegger, M. Cited in Magill, F.N. and Rodriguez J. (Eds) (1996) *International Encyclopedia of Psychology*. London: Fitzroy Dearborn Publishers.

Wehr, T. Symbolism of place (day and night). http://www.symbolism.org/writing/books/sp/4/page3.html (June 21,

2011).

Weiss, R. (1999). Sixth sense: it's not all in the mind. *The Age* (Melbourne), 7 May, 1999, pp86–87.

'What? Me Worry!?!' www.cci.health.wa.gov.au/resources/infopax.cfm?Info_ID=46 (March 30, 2011).

Wilde, S. (2001) *Miracles*. Carlsbad, CA: Hay House.

Willis, J. (February 6, 2010) Why Healthy Teenagers Die. http://www.psychologytoday.com/blog/radical-teaching/201002/why-healthy-teenagers-die (March 7, 2011).

Young, L. (26 February 2007) *Suicide Statistics Statement,* CEO beyondblue. www.beyondblue.org.au (February 14, 2011).

Young, L. Suicide Statistics. *beyondblue: the national depression initiative*. Based on *Reporting Suicide and Mental Illness*, C/W of Aust. (2002) and Australian Bureau of Statistics – *Suicides 1994–2004,* Catalogue Number 3309 (2006). www. beyond blue.org.au (February 14, 2011).

'Znakharka: The Knowing Ones'. Phillips, Sarah D. Waxing Like the Moon: Women Folk Healers in Rural Western Ukraine. *Folklorica: Journal of the Slavic and East European Folklore Association*. University of Indiana (May 1, 2011).

Zolota, Pavilina. Magic New Moon Spell. Cited in Phillips, S.D. Waxing Like the Moon: Women Folk Healers in Rural Western Ukraine. *Folklorica: Journal of the Slavic and East European Folkore Association. ISSN 1920-0242*. Electronic article hosted by the Center for Digital Scholarship, University of Kansas Libraries. https://journals.ku.edu/index.php/folklorica/article/viewFile/3744/3583 (April 5, 2011).